A Christology
of Peace

A Christology of Peace

James E. Will

Westminster/John Knox Press
Louisville, Kentucky

© 1989 James E. Will

Scripture quotations from the Revised Standard Version of the Bible are copyrighted 1946, 1952, © 1971, 1973 by the Division of Christian Education of the National Council of the Churches of Christ in the U.S.A. and are used by permission.

Book design by Peter Gall

First edition

Published by Westminster/John Knox Press
Louisville, Kentucky

PRINTED IN THE UNITED STATES OF AMERICA
9   8   7   6   5   4   3   2   1

Library of Congress Cataloging-in-Publication Data

Will, James E.
 A christology of peace / James E. Will. — 1st. ed.
      p.   cm.
 ISBN 0-8042-0540-X

 1. Jesus Christ—Person and offices.   2. Peace—Religious aspects—Christianity.   I. Title
 BT205.W48 1989   89-31790
 232′.8—dc20   CIP

Contents

Preface

This work is the result of long meditation on the crucial importance and immense difficulty of adequately expressing the Christian meaning of peace. It is written by someone whose whole personal and professional experience has been marked by the churches' increasing effort to witness to the meaning of Christ's peace during a cold war of superpowers armed with nuclear weapons and hot wars fought in Korea, Vietnam, Afghanistan, and almost everywhere else in what we have dared to call the "third world." In addition to my work of teaching systematic theology and theological ethics while helping direct the Peace and Justice Center of Garrett-Evangelical Theological Seminary, I have been privileged to reflect on the work of the Board of Global Ministries of the United Methodist Church, the Chicago Area Faculty for a Freeze (CAFF), the Christian Peace Conference (CPC), Christians Associated for Relationships with Eastern Europe (CAREE), the Churches' Human Rights Programme for the Implementation of the Helsinki Final Act, Clergy and Laity Concerned (CALC), the Inter-unit Committee on International Concerns of the National Council of the Churches of Christ in the U.S.A., and the United Nations Association, in all of which I have been privileged to have some responsibility.

The Christology of peace here articulated has grown out of the conviction that simpler forms of expressing the meaning of peace through a "Jesusology" based only on the ethical teachings of the historical Jesus have proven to be inadequate. Though the

churches' "dangerous memory" of the historical Jesus is crucial to
our faith, only a full-orbed Christology can provide an adequate
basis for understanding our personal experience of peace or our
social witness and activity for peace. The message of peace too
simply proclaimed in what we have come to call the "social gospel"
is neither sufficiently social nor an adequate gospel. The gospel
interpreted by the church in the last decade of the twentieth century must provide a more comprehensive understanding of peace
if it is to be genuinely good news for so complex and conflicted a
world as ours has become.

Nothing less than a full Christology of peace will suffice. That
is, the issues that the church has sought to clarify through its faith
in Jesus as the Christ must provide a paradigm for our interpretation of the Christian meaning of peace. Our understanding of peace
must interpret, and our work for peace must express, how our
humanity may ultimately be united with God's eternal wisdom and
purpose. My conviction is that only a fully trinitarian theology is
sufficient for attempting to articulate what Christians mean by
either social or gospel as we work for peace. A fully trinitarian
Christology illumines our ethical struggle for peace in a peaceless
world as the gracious gift of participation in the power and pathos
of the trinitarian life of our Creator and Redeemer. Since many
Christians become disillusioned because of a much simpler understanding of the possibility of peace, the articulation of such a
Christology is essential to sustain the peace work and witness of
the ecumenical churches.

After stating the issue of the universality of peace in dialectical
tension with the particularity of all of our human understandings
of peace in the first chapter, chapters 2 through 4 develop the
rudiments of a Christology of peace by interpreting the Jewishness,
crucifixion, and resurrection of Jesus in relation to the struggle for
a dialectical peace in the Spirit and spirit of peace. In these chapters
I am indebted to the monumental exegetical and hermeneutical
work of Edward Schillebeeckx above all, the philosophical theological insights of Paul Tillich and process theologians like John B.
Cobb, Jr., and Daniel Day Williams, and the political theological
wisdom of Jürgen Moltmann and liberation theologians like Leonardo Boff.

The theological integration of these insights into a Christology that might guide the churches' peace witness and action is developed in chapters 5 and 6. Seeking to articulate a synthesis and indicate its concrete relevance, these chapters are longer than the earlier chapters. The perspective that governs the whole analysis also becomes more explicit here, though it is clearly implicit throughout. Since all theology is contextual and perspectival, what is offered here is clearly only *a* Christology of peace. It is offered, however, with the prayerful hope that it may contribute to *the* theology of peace that the Holy Spirit is leading the ecumenical church dialogically to articulate in our thermonuclear era.

While offering it to the church, I dedicate it to my children: Kristen, Laurie, Michael, Eric, and Kevin. Much of the motivation for my work, like many other parents of my generation, has been the concern that they too might have a world in which to grow to full maturity so as to experience and make their own commitments to Christ's peace. They also have known, however, the fragility of familial peace at home while engaged in the social struggles to make our world a safer home for humanity. The maturity they, and many others in their generation, have achieved in their continuing commitments to universal peace with justice is one of God's greatest gifts to my peace.

J.E.W.

1

The Universality of God and the Particularity of Peace

To know Jesus as the Christ is to receive through him what only God can give—a power so creative that it brings creatures in all of their complexity and conflict to completion. It is to experience in and through him, and the communities that derive from him, what all personal therapies and social revolutions seek, and sometimes approximate, but never fully achieve. Yet we hardly know what we mean when we frame so comprehensive a thought. How can incomplete persons in an unfinished history know what the fulfillment of their personal and social lives might be? And if we ever experience so creative a power, can we recognize and name it? Could the symbols or concepts we use to name and understand it ever be adequate for its characterization?

Mystery and Complexity

Despite every danger of distortion caused by approaching Christ through our human needs, all forms of christological affirmation are related to our human aspirations for fulfillment. We human beings cannot cease seeking and thinking in terms of what we believe contributes to our happiness, or healing, or maturity, or enlightenment, or blessedness, or salvation. To experience weakness is to seek strength; to be lonely is to desire intimacy; to fear ignorance is to want truth; to suffer personal division and social divisiveness is to long for wholeness; to suffer oppression is to seek liberty; to endure conflict is to want harmony; to face death is to seek life. In the midst of our suffering and struggle we may not be able fully to characterize the completion we need and seek, but there are vectors in our experience pointing us toward what we must consider our salvation.

The most obvious of our human needs are basic and universal; all of us need food and shelter. For many, a modicum of technique transmitted through the culture of a functioning society meets these basic needs. But not always! The hunger and even starvation in our contemporary world, where many societies are in transition from subsistence agriculture to market-oriented agribusiness, do not allow this to be taken for granted. Millions are reduced to struggle for their next meal, and tens of thousands each day lose that struggle to death. Basic shelter also is not available to millions of economic refugees, moving from village to urban slum, or to military refugees driven from their homes by myriad conflicts. The foci of hope for people who have been driven to the very margins of human society must take the elemental forms of meeting basic needs, sometimes through deliverance from those social forces that cause their deprivation and drive them to desperation.

Hundreds of millions of others of us are more fortunate. Our social and economic possibilities in more prosperous societies allow us to focus on other values. Education opens vast cultural realms to us. A growing technology increasingly facilitates our pursuit of them. Instant communication and rapid travel now make possible even cross-cultural experiences, bridging many national and social barriers. What in early experience is a neighborhood becomes in maturity a national society, and today for some may even begin to approximate a human world. Until hampered by illness or limited by age, we seek an ever-expanding historical fulfillment: a broader knowledge, a richer aesthetic experience, a wider community. But even we must finally seek a more comprehensive meaning that will include death, our own, and ultimately all that we have learned to value.

In the midst of the mystery of such complexity, millions of human beings have experienced Jesus as mediating the power of God, a power so ultimate that it can bring to completion not only our finite creatureliness but that of all creation. It is inevitable that such ultimate power will be comprehended under many metaphors: to the hungry, Christ shall be bread; to the homeless, refuge; to the oppressed, liberation; to the culturally privileged, truth, beauty, and community; to the sick, healing; and to the dying, resurrection.

Religious symbols and theological concepts have sought to gather this whole range of meaning under more comprehensive terms, like the widely used "salvation." The meaning of these comprehensive concepts, however, is inevitably differentiated by the felt needs of those being "saved," and such needs are always relative to their emotional maturity, intellectual sophistication, and social status. Our theological understanding of the salvation we seek, and perhaps partially experience, is inevitably conditioned by our place in a particular society.

Peace as a Meaning of Salvation

The personal and social relativity sketched above especially affects the long tradition that has sought to understand salvation in terms of "peace," whether the *shalom* of Israel in the Hebrew scriptures (Pss. 125:5 and 128:6); the *eirene* of Christ in the New Testament (Col. 3:15); the *pax* of Augustine in the Roman Empire (*The City of God,* XIX. 12); the confession of Allah as "the All-holy, the All-peace" (Qur'an 59:23); or the benedictions pronounced as the completion of almost every Christian liturgy.

It is not surprising that this symbol achieved larger currency during periods of greater danger and insecurity. The Hebrew prophets expressed their most powerful visions of *shalom* during the eighth and seventh centuries B.C.E., when Israel faced devastation and deportation from the Assyrian and Babylonian empires. The evangelists of the New Testament witnessed to Jesus mediating an *eirene* that their "world could not give" just when Rome was destroying Jerusalem because of the Zealot revolt. And Augustine focused on *pax* as Rome itself was falling to the Goths, bringing centuries of the *pax Romana* to an end. He wrote at that perilous time in a way that many Christians since have found fits all times:

> Whoever gives moderate attention to human affairs and to our common nature will recognize that even as there is no

one who does not wish to be joyful, neither is there anyone
who does not wish to have peace.[1]

The power of peace as a religious symbol reaches far beyond its
sociopolitical meaning, however, to the deeply personal issues of
the human self. The depth psychologists of our century have rear-
ticulated the intrapsychic conflicts that religious sensitivity has
long expressed in terms of the guilt of a divided soul, the demonic
bondage of the soul possessed by alien powers, or the despair of a
soul lost in its own "dark night." To know the turbulence of a
troubled self is to know the dialectical opposite of the spiritual
peace that many, if not all, seek. Thus, millions, in good times and
bad, have responded to the promise of the resurrected Christ:
"Peace I leave with you; my peace I give to you; not as the world
gives do I give to you. Let not your hearts be troubled, neither let
them be afraid" (John 14:27).

Peace may function in the Judaeo-Christian tradition as so comprehensive a symbol because its meaning is rooted in the concept
of wholeness. The prophetic vision of *shalom* foresaw a society
where the needs of every person would be satisfied in a covenant
between God and persons and nature. The *personal* peace of "everyone under his vine and fig tree" is joined with the *social* peace
of nations not "learning war any more" (Mic. 4:3–4) and the
natural peace of the "wolf dwelling with the lamb" (Isa. 11:6). This
comprehensive meaning of peace came to its climax in Second
Isaiah's vision of the suffering love that "made us whole" (Isa.
53:5), where the word properly translated "whole" is *shalom.* The
proper meaning of *shalom* implies personal and social wholeness.

This biblical meaning of peace, however, is often the dialectical
opposite of the historical and personal reality portrayed in the very
same Bible. The breakdown of tribal peace in Israel's early history
is portrayed in Genesis, when Joseph is sold into Egyptian slavery
because his brothers no longer could "speak *shalom*" to him (Gen.
37:4). The dissolution of national peace after a brief epoch of
Davidic glory is told in the long history of national decline and
defeat following the division of the kingdom, because of the extrav-
agance of King Solomon and the injustice of King Rehoboam (1
Kings 7–12).

On the more personal plane, Israel's prophets sometimes had to
declare that no one could be found "who does justice and seeks

truth" (Jer. 5:1). Even Christ's apostles are portrayed in the New Testament, especially in the Gospel of Mark, as spiritually incapable of understanding him, so that in Jesus' time of trial and death, "they all forsook him, and fled" (Mark 14:50). Paul, the apostle known best because the New Testament contains so many of his pastoral letters, candidly confesses his personal struggle in not doing "the good I want, but the evil I do not want is what I do" (Rom. 7:19).

Human Limits and God's Peace

The human failure to achieve either the peace of personal integrity or social harmony is vividly recounted again and again in the Judaeo-Christian scriptures. Christians, nevertheless, have sought to express the meaning of Jesus for them over twenty centuries in the affirmation that "he is our peace" (Eph. 2:14). Given our human need, it is no wonder that we have looked to Christ for this great gift; but by the same token, it is also to be understood that they, and we, have often misinterpreted the peace we have received in highly particularistic ways, distorted by the alienations and conflicts of our particular contexts.

Our human limits in expressing Christ's peace may be seen even in their earliest expression in the New Testament, as in the way that the resolution of the long-standing conflict between the Jews and the Greeks was formulated. Jews had known deep conflict with Greeks since the Seleucids, after the conquests of Alexander the Great, had sought to impose Greek culture and religion upon them, even to the extreme of compelling the worship of Zeus in the Jerusalem temple dedicated to YHWH. The Hasmoneans/Maccabeans had fought a long and finally victorious war to liberate them from this oppression. Nevertheless, Greek culture was rich and in many ways attractive, so that hellenistic Jews knew the struggle between Hebraic faith and Greek culture in their very souls. It is no wonder that first-century Christians received and interpreted the peace of Christ as overcoming this deep division. Paul could exult with the church in Galatia, "There is neither Jew nor Greek . . . ; for you are all one in Christ Jesus" (Gal. 3:28). And the Christians in Ephesus saw the basis for their social peace in Christ:

> For he is our peace, who has made us both one, and has
> broken down the dividing wall of hostility, by abolishing in
> his flesh the law of commandments and ordinances, that he
> might create in himself one new man in place of the two, so
> making peace.
>
> Ephesians 2:14–15

Yet this very way of understanding their peace, so attractive
especially to hellenistic Jews living in the diaspora, bore the seeds
of a continuing, and even heightened, conflict with the Jews and
Jewish Christians, who understood their everlasting covenant with
God to be mediated through their law (the Torah). How could
"abolishing" the Torah of YHWH—as expressed in Ephesians
above and elsewhere (cf. Gal. 5:18)—contribute to ultimate peace
between Jews and Greeks? How could the universal peace brought
by a Jewish Jesus be created on the basis of so conflictual a stance
toward the religious foundation of his and their Jewish brothers
and sisters?

The "Common Declaration" of Professor Pinchas Lapide, an
Orthodox Israeli Jew, and Professor Jürgen Moltmann, a Protestant theologian of the University of Tübingen, after their dialogue
in West Germany in 1978, puts this issue so poignantly that no
Christian should be able to evade it:

> The tragedy of Christian-Jewish relations lies above all in the
> fact that Jesus of Nazareth, who should have been "our
> peace" (Eph. 2:14)—a bridge of reconciliation between Israel
> and the world of the nations—has become a trench of hostil-
> ity. . . . When the teacher and the (later) teaching, the
> preacher and the praxis separate from one another so terri-
> bly, when the good news of the Christians could become the
> sad news of the Jews, we should pluck up our courage so as
> to place before us the basic questions: . . . Where is it really
> the Lord, the Eternal One our God, who separates us in all
> that which for so long has split and alienated Christians and
> Jews? And where is it we, with our handiwork and our
> human thoughts, who set up barriers and hinder a rapproche-
> ment?[2]

A theological perspective that helps answer these questions will
be articulated at length in the next chapter. But the questions are
introduced here to show that Christians, as they sought personal

and social peace, have had great difficulty from the very beginning in receiving and expressing God's peace through Jesus in ways that contribute toward a genuinely universal peace.

The long and tragic history of Christian-Jewish relations requires very careful formulation of the Christology of peace at this foundational point if it is not to contribute to continuing anti-Semitism. Christian theologies that claim, or even leave any room for the implication, that Christianity has displaced and superseded Judaism cannot contribute to the peace of Christ. Chapter 2 will examine the basis for Christian peace in the apostolic interpretation of a Jewish Jesus which discerns theological continuity with Judaism and finds the basis for the universalization of Christianity through the Jewish Wisdom tradition.

We need not trace the history of Christendom in detail to recall that the peace of Christ has often been distorted by other interpretations affected by the conflicted contexts of our churches. The very fact that we must use the word "church" in the plural indicates that we have not always received a sufficient grace to maintain peace within the Christian community itself. Thus the first Christian writing on "irenology" was addressed to just this issue of ecumenism, to restore peace and unity to the church. Our churches have not only been differentiated but deeply divided by national loyalties, sometimes legally formalized by actually assuming the status of a "state church." Even in states enjoying religious tolerance and freedom, denominational differentiation has been marked and marred by racial and ethnic divisions and class stratification.[3]

The Inevitability of Ideology

The divisiveness of our history is enough to convince many Christian thinkers that there is an inevitable ideological factor in any of our understandings of Jesus as the Christ.[4] That is, there is a factor, even if often unconscious, of self-interest and group interest in the complex of feelings, attitudes, evaluations, and ideas that affects every theological formulation of Jesus' meaning for human salvation. And when "peace" is the symbol used to appropriate and express our salvation, this ideological factor is often heightened and always more dangerous. The contemporary German theologian Wolfhart Pannenberg has therefore concluded that a separation between Christology and soteriology is not possible, because in general the soteriological interest, the interest in salvation, in the *beneficia Christi,* is what causes us to ask about the figure of Jesus. . . . However, the danger that is involved in this connection between Christology and soteriology has emerged at the same time: Has one really spoken there about Jesus himself at all? . . . Do not the desires of men only become projected upon the figure of Jesus, personified in him? . . . The danger that Christology will be *constructed* out of the soteriological interest ought to be clear.[5]

The Christian theological ethicist Gibson Winter has also addressed this concern by examining whether it may be transcended by using the modern methodology of social science. He examined the work of sociologists like Talcott Parsons and C. Wright Mills to identify the scientific aspects that may be common to a variety of objective considerations of society. He had to conclude, however, that ideology was inevitable even in the work of social scientists:

They follow to differing degrees the procedures of the empirical sciences, and they attempt, so far as possible, to give a reliable interpretation of their findings. So far as these scientists suffer ideological strains, and all to varying degrees undergo such strain, this is perhaps the human condition.[6]

Ideology is an inevitable dimension of our human condition, because we are finite, social, incomplete, and estranged selves. There is no objective scientific methodology that enables us fully to escape this condition. So when we think theologically about issues of ultimate concern like salvation and peace, we hardly dare hope entirely to escape the self- and group interests that inevitably affect our thought.

The ideological strain in all thought, including theology, may be more readily accepted as inevitable when we understand that we are social selves, constituted in part by the relationships we have intimately experienced. The security and stimulus provided by a family is the necessary context for our personal growth and individuation. The varying degrees of tension, rejection, and even abuse in these intimate relations, however, are the climate of anxiety in which our personal distortions and estrangement also emerge and develop. Deep patterns of affirmation and rejection of self and others developed in early intimate relationships, of moving toward or away from or against other persons, of adversion toward or aversion from various values, of basic trust and distrust, hope and despair, continue to affect feeling, thought, and action long after we have moved into larger spheres of relationships in communities, schools, churches, and the world. We may transcend these early patterns through personal growth in later creative contexts, but the continuity of unconscious and conscious memories in our personal histories allows for no complete transcendence. The child remains parent to the adult in us all.[7]

For this reason, the "honoring of father and mother" in the Mosaic sixth commandment does not only have moral significance; it also has a deeper theological meaning, directly related to the earlier Mosaic commandments that specify our relation to God our Creator. God concretely creates us through the biological and social processes we experience in relation to our families. It is thus impossible to worship our Creator without honoring our parents. No matter what personal inadequacies or distortions we may later think traceable to deficiencies in the way we have been parented, our family is still the primary context of grace through which we have been given our existence. Using a paraphrase of an affirmation sometimes made soteriologically about the church, we may assert ontologically that no one can have God for their Abba ("father" in Jesus' terms) who does not have the family for his or her mother.

What is primarily true for a family becomes secondarily true for the culture of a society. A social culture is the necessary context for personal growth. The technique, science, literature, art, and religion of a culture complete what a family can only begin. Whatever the structures of formal and informal education a culture provides, they are essential to educing what otherwise would remain only potential within us. The degree of intellectual, aesthetic, and spiritual maturity we realize remains strictly relative to the richness of the culture in which we are privileged to participate.

Unfortunately for many, the degree of access to the richness of their culture is conditioned by the social status and economic possibilities of their families and the democratic openness of their society. In larger, more complex societies, racial and ethnic factors also often prejudice the scope of opportunity. But however power-

ful these class and racial limitations may be, everyone finally recognizes their dependence upon their given culture for the fulfillment
of their lives. It is perhaps the opportunity to live for a time in
another social culture or the difficulty of living in a highly pluralistic culture that enables a person most sharply to realize how much
of his or her identity is given by the culture in which he or she has
matured.

The history of humanity to the present has made nations and
nation-states the principal contexts for the development of culture.
There are, of course, families of nations that share a common
language and thus many other elements of culture. But especially
since the emergence of sovereign states in the northern hemisphere
after feudalism, and the transfer of this political pattern to the
southern hemisphere through colonialism, the nation-state has
become the principal bearer of culture.

The dependence upon culture for personal fulfillment in the
context of contemporary nationalism explains the inevitable ideological strain even in our theological sense of "peace." The peace
of personal integration requires some sense of harmony with the
social wholes of family and society in which we have come to being.
As social selves, we cannot know, or even approximate, any wholeness of being which is personal peace, apart from achieving some
kind of peace with the concrete context to which we are internally
related. No matter what degree of spiritual transcendence over
family and society is later realized, every self-transcendent person
remains continuous with the self created first within a national
culture. Our experience and expression of "peace" will inevitably
remain relative to the national culture through which we have
partially been given our being. Thus national particularity will
inevitably characterize even our most universal affirmations of
peace.

Many "nationalists," of course, have no difficulty in recognizing
and affirming this reality. They expect peace only within national
borders, which must be drawn and protected precisely for the sake
of peace. To the extent that they see peace dependent upon factors
beyond their national borders, it must be secured by diplomatically
or, if necessary, militarily extending the economic and political
power of their state. In this nationalistic view, war is a possible

instrument of peace, as the extension of national diplomacy by other means. From a nationalist perspective, any threat to one's state is an enemy of peace, and any means finally necessary to the removal or neutralization of this threat is in the service of peace.

Enmity Is the Enemy of Universal Peace

Any nationalistic understanding of peace, however, is profoundly incoherent with belief in the universal God. All monotheistic faith moves beyond nationalism toward concern for universal peace. Despite all contrary ideological tendencies, the peace of God in the love of Christ directs Christians toward more universal community.

The character of Christian commitment to universal peace has its clearest expression in the memory of Jesus' most distinctive teaching, preserved in the Q source of Matthew's and Luke's Gospels: "Love your enemies and pray for those who persecute you" (Matt. 5:44 and Luke 6:35). The threat to any particular peace is in some sense enemy, but the threat to universal peace is *enmity* itself. Universal peace may be achieved and sustained only by transforming all enmity. It is precisely the love of all enemies that finally vanquishes enmity.

God's universal gracious relation to the whole creation is the theological context in which Jesus set his teaching of the love of enemies:

> Love your enemies and pray for those who persecute you, so that you may be children of your Abba who is in heaven; for he makes his sun rise on the evil and on the good, and sends rain on the just and on the unjust. . . . You, therefore, must be perfect as your heavenly Abba is perfect.
>
> Matthew 5:44–48; cf. Luke 6:35–36
> (modified for inclusive language)

The notion of perfection here attributed to God and demanded of Christians is closely related to the biblical sense of *shalom.* Our particular human loves must finally be transformed by experience of God's universal love, which embraces the whole and makes it whole. The universal gracious love of God knows no limit set by human enmity. The limitation, negativity, and estrangement created in particularistic human relationships are transcended by God, who calls us to transcend them in God.[8]

The revelation of God in Jesus Christ has usually been interpreted theologically with the theme of "salvation history" that runs through the Bible. But this teaching of universal love of enemies illustrates that much of Jesus' message must also be interpreted within the blessing tradition, grounded in belief in God as the Creator, which also runs through the Hebrew and Christian scriptures.[9] God's redemptive activity, whether interpreted through the covenant with Israel or the new covenant through Jesus Christ as salvation history, must finally be understood within the context of God's creation and universal blessing of all humanity. The Bible's first book begins with the story of the establishment of blessing in creation (Gen. 1:26–27), and its concluding book ends with the reestablishment of a blessed world (Rev. 22:1–5).

In the creation-blessing tradition within scripture, God pushes back the powers of chaos to create and preserve an orderly world; and all human beings are created in the image of God, with the infinite dignity of participating in the preservation and completion of the creation. This ultimate dignity of being created in the *imago dei* is affirmed of all persons, quite apart from any national or cultural qualification. The subsequent differentiation of humanity by language, culture, and nation, as portrayed in Genesis 10–11, is the consequence of the human pride and pretension that so often blocks and distorts participation in God's creativity and limits or removes God's blessing (Gen. 11:6–9).

The Necessity of Praxis

If incomplete and ideologically distorted persons nevertheless have the dignity of participation with their Creator in the preservation and completion of the creation, then praxis is a necessary dimension of theology. But praxis must not be misunderstood as practice. Practice has come to mean the use of external means to attain a theoretically defined end. It suggests that finite and sinful persons may so understand the meaning of God's peace as to be able to devise economic, political, diplomatic, and even military means to attain it. The end of peace is thought to be a transcendent value that appropriate external means may effect.

Praxis, on the other hand, is a dialectical process of internally related events from which a result dynamically emerges. Given the finite and ideological character of our preconceptions of peace, they cannot be treated as sufficient definitions of an eternal value to guide our practice. Rather, we need a praxis; that is, peace must be allowed to emerge from a dialogical and dialectical process that may continuously correct our ideological tendencies. Praxis is thus a process of struggle, negotiation, and dialogue toward a genuinely voluntary consensus.

We shall discuss more completely in chapter 6 that kind of praxis which may allow the local church in each place, and particularly in North America, to participate in the world mission of the ecumenical church to co-create universal peace. Though my claim is not quite so bold as Frederick Herzog's in his *God-Walk,* this work fundamentally agrees with his position:

> Some dogmatics texts still begin from the premise that theory provides guidelines for walking in the world—for action. The project of liberation shaping dogmatics, by contrast, is premised on the inescapably conflictual context where praxis precedes theory. Dogmatics now is shown to arise out of God-walk.[10]

Divine Wisdom as the Basis for Universal Peace Praxis

In the Bible's universal Wisdom motif, grounded in faith in one God as universal creator, enmity is the evil to be overcome. The teaching in Hebrew Wisdom literature is that the enemy is to be met with care and concern: "If your enemy is hungry, give him bread to eat; and if he is thirsty, give him water to drink" (Prov. 25:21). Persons who share in God's universal creativity do not seek to vanquish the enemy but to transform enmity, so that God's image may be actualized in the wisdom of all human beings.

The portrayal and interpretation of Jesus in the New Testament, especially in the Q tradition, establishes a close connection between its picture of Jesus and the idea of Wisdom found in the late Hebraic Wisdom tradition. Though more detailed analysis shall be postponed until the next chapter, it may be pointed out here that, in the proverbs of the early hellenistic period, Wisdom was personified as brought forth from God before all creation and as working creatively beside God in all subsequent creation: "When he marked out the foundations of the earth, then I [Wisdom] was beside him, like a master workman; and I was daily his delight, rejoicing before him always" (Prov. 8:29–30; cf. Prov. 3:19 and Ps. 104:24). A more eschatological concept of Wisdom emerged during the Hasmonean/Maccabean period among the Chasidim, from whom came both the Pharisees and the Essenes active in the New Testament period. Chasidic wisdom was understood to give insight into the "last things," based on revelation from heavenly Wisdom (cf. Dan. 2:20–23 and *1 Enoch*). Although this chasidic conception of Wisdom was more historical and eschatological than the more ontological hellenistic notion of Wisdom as permeating the whole creation, both traditions understood heavenly Wisdom as providing the ultimate and final meaning of the whole creation.

Some of the New Testament's most ancient hymns use this notion of preexistent Wisdom to interpret the meaning of Jesus. Hebrews 1:2–4, Philippians 2:6–11, Colossians 1:15–20, and most clearly the prologue of the Gospel of John express Jesus' divine significance by symbols derived from this tradition:

> In the beginning was the Word, and the Word was with God, and the Word was God. He was in the beginning with God; all things were made through him, and without him was not anything made that was made. . . . And the Word became flesh and dwelt among us, full of grace and truth; we have beheld his glory, glory as of the only Son from the Father.
>
> John 1:1–3, 14

Although this Wisdom Christology became suspect to some because it might be linked to incipient gnosticism in the church, as may be seen already in Paul's response to the Corinthian church (cf. 1 Cor. 1:19–2:16), it nevertheless remained as the scriptural basis for the universalistic Logos Christology of the patristic period. This idea of the Logos/Word/Wisdom provided the essential conceptual bridge between Jesus of Nazareth and the God who is the universal creator of meaning and order, and who alone can bring creation to its ultimate completion.

Thus Christians came to affirm that it was the divine Logos in Jesus who gives us universal peace. Apart from the relation he mediates with the universal God, we cannot know any ultimate peace in our human history. Yet the ideological strains in the national and cultural particularities of our human existence make our reception of universal peace problematic, as became evident from the very beginning. Even the way in which it was received and expressed in the earliest apostolic communities, through whom we received our New Testament, shows this ideological distortion, as we already have noted in the arguments about the salvific meaning of the Jewish Torah. The inertia of their Jewish, Greek, and Roman histories resisted any more universal meaning. Habit, anxiety, and defensiveness distorted, and continue to distort, our human reception of the incarnation of God's universal gracious Logos.

This problematic of universal peace and historical particularity puts before us the very elements with which every theologian has had to work in understanding Christology. The issue always has been whether and how a fully particular person and, in Jesus' case, a fully Jewish man might "incarnate" the universal wisdom and peace of God. Because Christians experience Jesus as having done so, the further question is to what degree his Jewish and hellenistic disciples could receive and communicate this revelation of universal peace in our scripture without ideological distortion. The same issue continues down to our day: Can European or Russian or American or Asian or African Christians hope to receive the gift of universal peace from the Christ mediated through our scripture and interpreted within the traditions of our churches? Is it possible yet to hope that our human history may be brought to completion in universal peace through Christ's saving power? In a thermonuclear age poised on the brink of catastrophe, dare we believe in Jesus as the Christ? Could it be that he really was and is and will be "our peace"?

Our first step in answering these questions must be to come to terms with the Jewish particularity of Jesus. Tragically, some traditional Christology has incorporated an anti-Jewish dimension from the very beginning, which has contributed to the horror that Jesus' Jewish brothers and sisters have suffered in some "Christian" societies for two millennia.[11] Christology can be conceived in ways that constrict and distort our understanding of God's universal relation to all creation, and in its *adversus Judaeas* formulations it certainly has done so. In my theological judgment, it is impossible really to believe and fully to understand that God's universal peace was uniquely present in our human history in a fully human Jesus until and unless we can understand how that was possible in a fully Jewish Jesus. If Jesus was "very God of very God" united with "very man of very man," as our later creeds came to affirm, that man must have been fully and completely a Jewish man. No sophisticated interpretations of an "enhypostatic union,"[12] though its universalistic intention may be affirmed, may be allowed to confuse this historical reality.

If Jesus really mediates a universal peace, it must intend and include peace for the Jews. Can we begin so to understand Jesus? Is it possible to continue to understand him so, even in the twentieth century when Israel and the Middle East constitute one of the least peaceful areas in our entire world? I turn to these issues in the next chapter.

2

The Jewishness of Jesus and the Struggle for Peace

The startling historical fact that focuses our attention and requires our interpretation in this chapter is that a Jew who was executed by all who were duly constituted as religious and political authorities in his obscure corner of the Roman world continues to be affirmed by hundreds of millions as the Christ—the One who so mediates the power of the universal God that the entire creation may be brought to its intended completion. What is even more arresting is that this Jew who suffered a criminal's death, in what amounted to a prologue to the Roman destruction of Jerusalem a generation later (70 C.E.) and the resulting diaspora of his fellow Jews for 1900 years, is interpreted as having brought the possibility of universal peace to human history. The christological issue is nowhere put more sharply than in this juxtaposition of its terms: A Jew crucified in a Jerusalem soon also to be destroyed and dispersed is the One anointed by God to bring universal peace.

The Tragedy of Jerusalem

Elie Wiesel, the survivor of Auschwitz, has written of the Jerusalem again reconstituted as Israel's capital after 1900 years:

> Jerusalem: the face visible, yet hidden, the sap and blood of all that makes us live or renounce life. The spark flashing in the darkness, the murmur rustling through shouts of happiness and joy. A name, a secret. For the exiled a prayer. For

> all others a promise. Jerusalem: seventeen times destroyed,
> yet never erased. The symbol of survival. Jerusalem: the city
> which miraculously transforms man into a pilgrim; no one
> can enter it and go away unchanged.[1]

These evocative words face a photograph of Jerusalem with the
superscription of a text from Isaiah used by Jesus when he
"cleansed" the Jerusalem temple: "For my house shall be called a
house of prayer for all peoples" (Isa. 56:7; Mark 11:17). Wiesel's
words, the words of one who epitomizes the long suffering of the
Jewish people since Jesus, resonate for the Christian with remind-
ers of the Jewish Jesus who entered Jerusalem two millennia ago
to die and exited it utterly changed by his resurrection, which also
changed the possibilities for the peace of the whole world.

There is no place in this world where it is both more easy and
more difficult to believe this about Jesus than in contemporary
Jerusalem. Here the memory *(anamnesis)* of Jesus is palpable because one is in the same places where he passed. One may visit the
Temple Mount where he taught and acted so vigorously, Gethsemane where he prayed, Golgotha where he died, and the Holy Se-
pulchre, now empty, from which he rose. Yet the power of this
memory is matched by the paradox of its affirmed meaning. For
Jerusalem remains one of the more terribly divided, peaceless cities
on all the globe—not only within the wall of the Old City with its
almost quaint Muslim, Jewish, Armenian, and Christian quarters,
but in the far more dangerous division of Arab East Jerusalem and
Jewish West Jerusalem, with animosities unresolved since the war
of 1948 and exacerbated by the war of 1967 and the subsequent
annexation of some of the conquered Arab territory.

The direct challenge to Christian faith inscribed at the base of
the golden dome in the Mosque of Omar, sitting upon the Temple
Mount where the Jewish temple stood until 70 C.E., seems peculiarly appropriate in this place:

> O you people of the Book, overstep not bounds in your
> religion, and of God speak only the truth. The Messiah,
> Jesus, son of Mary, is only an apostle of God, and his Word
> which he conveyed into Mary, and a Spirit proceeding from
> him. Believe therefore in God and his apostles, and say not

> Three. It will be better for you. God is only one God. Far be
> it from his glory that he should have a son.

Here is expressed the Muslim reverence for Jesus as a prophet of
God, which is matched in the classrooms of Hebrew University on
neighboring Mount Scopus, where rabbis like Professor David
Flusser interpret Jesus as one of Judaism's greatest rabbis.[2] Yet
here is also the rejection of the Christian faith in Jesus as the Son
of God, the Logos/Wisdom of the Trinity become incarnate, the
definitive presence and action of God in human history to bring
creation to its completion in peace.

Any Christian faithful to Jesus must ask why any Muslim could
or should believe that Jesus brought the power of God's universal
peace into human history, after a history in which the Christian
Crusaders slaughtered every Muslim man, woman, and child upon
taking Jerusalem in 1099. And on the other side, Christians must
also ask why faithful Jews could or should affirm more about Jesus
than Professor Flusser already does, after the Holocaust, that culmination of 1900 years of anti-Semitism in "Christian" Europe.

The Apocalyptic Form of Jewish Faith in Jesus' Era

First, however, we must ask how a fully Jewish Jesus could
become the basis for a new world religion within five years after
his death by execution in Jerusalem. How is it that, only three years
after his crucifixion, a hellenistic Pharisee like Saul could be converted to faith in Jesus as the Christ while en route to Damascus
to persecute adherents of this new faith?

Jesus lived in that period of Jewish history, between the Has-
monean/Maccabean struggle begun in 167 B.C.E. and ended in the
Jewish wars of 63–73 C.E., which was spiritually dominated by
apocalyptic expectations and speculations. Many Jews had come to
feel that their lives could not endure much longer the indignity and
suffering caused by the present patterns of history, and thus they
both longed for and envisioned a radical change. Professor Pinchas
Lapide has written:

> Only in Hasmonean times, as the gruesome yoke of the Gen-
> tiles and the failure of their own leaders brought the people
> to the edge of despair, did there arise from the abyss of

suffering a vision of an anointed redeemer who as an ideal regent embodied truth and justice, and who was destined to restore the order of God in a world that had fallen out of joint.[3]

Only after the zealotry fueled by these apocalyptic hopes had led to the destruction of Jerusalem, with 6,000 Jews slaughtered in their temple while awaiting the last-minute arrival of their messiah, did this apocalypticism give way to that sober interpretation of the Torah we have known ever since under the leadership of at first pharasaic rabbis. Realists about the consequences of this war, like Rabbi Jochanan ben Sakkai, who had himself smuggled out of Jerusalem in a coffin while it was under siege in 70 C.E., negotiated with Vespasian the possibility of continuing Jewish life, centered first in Daphne in northern Galilee. Their rabbinic leadership allowed the resulting Jewish diaspora to survive under the guidance of the Torah, as interpreted by the emerging Mishna and Talmud.[4] The Zealots, however, fought to the end on the Temple Mount as they awaited the messiah in 70 C.E., and 900 others of them committed suicide on Masada in 73 C.E., as the Romans breached the defenses of this, their last fortress.

The images created in this apocalyptic tradition provided much of the religious symbolism current in Jesus' generation to thematize and interpret their faith and hope in God. Expectations of a kingly, priestly, or prophetic messiah, or a more mysterious celestial Son of Man, were the forms of their historical hope. The specific form of the historical existence of Jesus convinced some in his generation that their hopes for salvation through a radical renewal of history—if not a reversal—were fulfilled in his life, death, and resurrection. This faith in Jesus, however, was inevitably formed and interpreted by, and perhaps also hidden beneath, the religious symbols and ideas of that apocalyptic time.[5]

It is, however, Jesus' peculiar historical existence that was and remains the criterion for the selection and transformation of the symbols and ideas used to interpret him. Thus Christian theology must constantly, critically seek to uncover the reality of Jesus communicated through these eschatological and apocalyptic symbols.

The gradual separation of the nascent Christian congregations from the synagogues led by the Pharisees, culminating in the rejection of these early Christians as no longer authentically Jewish, led to a polemical response to the synagogues that Jesus, of course, never experienced or intended—at least in the form that it later took. This polemic seriously complicated the New Testament church's interpretation of the Jewish Jesus. It must no longer be allowed, however, to disguise or distort the truth that "the early Christian interpretation of Jesus is really a Jewish one"[6]—which is also to say that the early Christian critique of Israel is also to be basically understood as an internal Jewish critique.

Jesus Received and Interpreted as the Eschatological Prophet

The first response to Jesus' teaching ministry already during his lifetime was that he was a "prophet." But to be judged a prophet in his era was extraordinary. The experience of Israel had led to the judgment among many that prophecy had come to an end, not to be renewed until the dawn of the messianic age (1 Macc. 9:27). Thus their messianic hope took the form of expecting an eschatological prophet, usually a prophet *redivivus* like Elijah or perhaps Jeremiah. It is quite clear that the identification of Jesus as this eschatological prophet was not a post-Easter reflection about him, because the same primitive Christian tradition also records that John the Baptist too was being interpreted as Elijah *redivivus* (Mark 9:13). Mark 6:14–16 and 8:28 embody perhaps the earliest interpretation of Jesus in this eschatological form: Jesus was understood to be Elijah or "one of the prophets of old" (Mark 6:15). The superstitious and guilty King Herod, who had beheaded John, was remembered as having even thought Jesus might be John returned to life.

What was this idea of the eschatological prophet, and how was it related to the church's later messianic interpretation of Jesus?

The Meanings of Messiah

In early Hebraic practice, only the king was anointed. Thus he alone was *mashiach,* messiah, YHWH's anointed one. As such, he also was named "Son of God" (Psalms 2 and 89). YHWH's promise and power was mediated through him for the blessing of Israel.

After the fall of the kingdom and the beginning of the Exile, however, the priests and then the prophets were also installed in office by anointing (1 Kings 19:16, Ps. 105:15). The prophet was thereby designated a "man of the Spirit," and to anoint him signified "passing on the prophetic Spirit" (cf. Hos. 9:7; Isa. 48:16; Ezek. 2:2, 11:5).

The authors of Deuteronomy, disenchanted with the kings of the Northern Kingdom and completing their work in the Southern Kingdom after the northern leaders had gone into Assyrian exile, began the process of humanizing the ideal of a Davidic kingly messiah with a prophetic Mosaic image as the ideal of a royal messiah. In this more prophetic messianism, *mashiach* came to mean the prophet filled with God's Spirit (Zech. 7:8–12). During and after the Exile, Israel began to look less to an idealized past, which had actually so often failed even to approximate their religious ideal, and began to look toward a promised future. Some of the oracles from Second and Third Isaiah (Second during and Third after the Exile) were especially important in defining the eschatological prophet as that one who would inaugurate this new age of God's blessing:

Behold my *servant,* whom I uphold,
  my *chosen,* in whom my soul delights;
I have put my Spirit upon him,
  he will bring forth justice to the nations.

How beautiful upon the mountains
  are the feet of him who brings good tidings,
who publishes peace, who brings good tidings of good,
  who publishes salvation,
  who says to Zion, "Your God reigns."

The Spirit of the Lord GOD is upon me,
  because the LORD has *anointed* me
to bring good tidings to the afflicted;
  he has sent me to bind up the brokenhearted,
to proclaim liberty to the captives,
  and the opening of the prison to those who are bound;
to proclaim the year of the LORD's favor,
  and the day of vengeance of our God.
                              Isaiah 42:1; 52:7; 61:1–2 (italics added)

Texts like these in the Judaism of Jesus' time provided the basis for their expectation of an "eschatological prophet," a prophetic messiah anointed by God, filled with God's Spirit, to bring the good news of God's approaching kingdom of justice and peace. Essene manuscripts discovered in Cave 4 at Qumran have shown that anthologies of such texts were brought together in late Judaism to express the basis for their messianic hope. The scroll found at Qumran peculiarly developed the idea of a dual messiah—both a priestly and a royal Davidic one. This form of messianic hope had led the Essenes of Qumran to join the Zealots in the war against Rome and thus had led to the destruction of their community after the fall of Jerusalem in 70 C.E..

Yet, as we have noted before, many others in the Judaism of Jesus' era thought this prophetic period had come to an end. We read in 1 Maccabees 9:27 a reference to "the time that prophets ceased to appear." Thereafter and therefore, the scribes took over the prophet's function of interpreting God's will, no longer by discerning the signs of the times but by interpreting the sacred texts, especially the Torah. The great hermeneutical process of creating *halakha* (law) and *haggada* (interpretative stories), which continues down to the orthodox rabbis of our own day, had thereby begun. In this scribal, spiritual movement, even the great prophets were subordinated to the Torah, the Books of Moses. Moses became the ideal type: king, legislator, priest, and prophet all in one. Philo of Alexandria wrote of Moses: "He was subsumed into the divine, so that he became akin to God, and truly godlike."[7]

Moreover, on the basis of Deuteronomy 17, those who sat on the seat of Moses, the high priest and the Sanhedrin in Jesus' time, were the religious establishment who alone could finally determine whether a Jew was good or presumptuously evil in the sight of YHWH (cf. esp. Deut. 17:12). Any kind of charismatic, prophetic activity, like that of Jesus or John the Baptist, could very well appear to be a provocative and presumptuous threat to this form of scribal, legal spirituality.

Despite the political predominance of this form of scribalism in association with King Herod, a charismatic interpretation of the prophets in an apocalyptic perspective nevertheless had grown during the century preceding Jesus. Circles inspired by this apocalyptic hermeneusis looked for an eschatological savior. Some looked for a royal messianic figure, a new David. Others looked for a latter-day messianic prophet. All looked for a radical transformation of the old world or eon into a new one. Many of these charismatic, apocalyptic expositions were written pseudonymously in the names of great leaders of the past: Moses, David, Enoch, Elijah. Especially those who had been "carried up" before or after death to be with God—Enoch, Elijah, and Moses—were favored sources. Malachi is one of the early anonymous collections of such oracles that was later accepted into the Hebrew canon; some of its representative texts that became important are: "Behold, I send my messenger to prepare the way before me" (Mal. 3:1) and "Behold, I send you Elijah the prophet before the great and terrible day of the LORD comes" (Mal. 4:5). A charismatic interpretation of Deuteronomy 18:15–18 also promised the coming of a latter-day "prophet like Moses," as another form of eschatological savior figure to inaugurate the new age.

The Universal Reign of YHWH and Royal Messianism

What was finally at stake in all of this for Jewish faith was the universal rule of YHWH over his whole creation. The Hebrew psalms often gave exultant expression to their faith that "God is the king of all the earth" (Ps. 47:7).

> For the LORD is a great God,
>   and a great King above all gods.
> In his hand are the depths of the earth;
>   the heights of the mountains are his also.
> The sea is his, for he made it;
>   for his hands formed the dry land.
> O come, let us worship and bow down,
>   let us kneel before the LORD, our Maker!
>   Psalm 95:3–6

It was this profound faith in YHWH as creator of the whole universe that provided the religious basis for the belief that God himself shall rule over the whole at last.

Many in Israel, of course, hoped that God would rule through his royal servant, their anointed king. After the division and fall of the Davidic dynasty, and especially after the Assyrian and Babylonian exiles, this hope took the form of expecting an eschatological royal messiah, a David *redivivus.* This hope was grounded in the prophecies of Isaiah (9:1–6 and 11:1–10), Jeremiah (23:5–6 and 33:15–16) and Micah (5:1–3); and it received later but disappointed expression in specific relation to Zerubbabel in Haggai (2:20–23) and to Joshua in Zechariah (6:9–15). Zechariah's oracle of the triumphal entry of the king-messiah into Jerusalem (9:9–10) also was important in this regard, not only because of its use in the New Testament to interpret Jesus' entry into Jerusalem but especially for the purposes of our study, because it prophesied that the messiah "shall command peace to the nations; his domain shall be from sea to sea, and from the River to the ends of the earth" (9:10).

During the Maccabean period in the century preceding Jesus, this royal messianic hope grew especially among the chasidic Pharisees and Essenes, because they could not accept the Hasmonean dynasty's having made themselves both kings and high priests, though they were not of the tribe of Judah. From their understanding of the Torah, it was blasphemy for any not of the tribe of Judah to make himself king. The Essenes of Qumran therefore turned to an eschatological priestly messianism in opposition to the Hasmoneans, and the Pharisees espoused a royal Davidic messianism. Both forms of these hopes seem to have come together in the late stages of the Qumran community, in their hope for both a royal and priestly messiah. But in the last stages, during the rebellious years under Herod the Great's son, Archelaus (4 B.C.E.–6 C.E.) and the Roman procurators that followed him in Judea (6–70 C.E.), when the Scroll of War was written, the hope for the royal messiah took precedence and led the Essenes to share in the disastrous rebellion that brought their destruction.

This revival of royal messianism in Jesus' era also gave rise to the nationalist freedom fighters, the Sicarri and the Zealots, who finally brought Israel to the brink of destruction in their revolt against Rome. In their faith, YHWH alone could rule over Israel. The Roman occupation after Pompey conquered the Hasmoneans (63 B.C.E.) was not only a national affront to them but a religious blasphemy. The collaboration of the Herodians, who ruled as vassals of Rome, and that of the Sadducees, the high priestly party collaborating with the Herodians, was an abomination. The moral resistance of the Pharisees was acceptable, but deemed insufficient and ineffective. The Zealots and Sicarri thus turned to violent subversive resistance. They knew their force was woefully insufficient against Rome, but on the basis of their charismatic interpretation of royal messianic passages, they counted on the advent of the messiah to complete what they could only begin.[8]

Richard Horsley's social history is persuasive in arguing that there was no organized group called the Zealots until the coalition that emerged in Jerusalem during the rebellion in the winter of 67–68 C.E. Thus he is technically correct that the Zealot movement should not be used as a foil for defining the position of Jesus a generation earlier, as Oscar Cullmann, Martin Hengel, and S. G. F. Brandon have attempted. Horsley's conviction is also persuasive that much of the discussion of "Jesus and the Zealots" ideologically obscures that Jesus actually advocated active resistance to the established order.[9]

Though there may not have been a group called the Zealots until 67 C.E., Horsley is as clear as other historians that there were active rebellions in Jesus' historical period, beginning with the outbreak of violent revolts in every major district of Herod's kingdom at his death in 4 B.C.E. Though Judas of Galilee and Saddok the Pharisee probably should not be considered founders of a Zealot movement and may have been basically nonviolent, they did advocate active tax resistance in 6 C.E., when Archelaus was deposed and Judea was to be directly governed by Rome. There also were massive popular demonstrations about 31 C.E. at the beginning of Pilate's rule in Judea, when he sent Roman legions into Jerusalem with standards that bore images of the emperor, which were considered a direct challenge to the ultimate sovereignty of YHWH over Judaism.

Solomonic-Sapiental Royal Messianism

It is one of the clearest aspects of the New Testament that Jesus rejected this zealotic form of royal messianism, as did the early Christian communities who worshiped and interpreted him as the Messiah. But there was another royal messianism of the "Son of David," which proved far more relevant as a background for Jesus' ministry and the church's earliest Christology. Here the image of the Son of David was derived from David's successor as king, his

son Solomon, to whom was attributed the whole Wisdom tradition
of Israel. First Kings 4:29–30 had affirmed that "God gave Solomon wisdom and understanding beyond measure . . . so that
Solomon's wisdom surpassed the wisdom of all of the people of the
east." Later pharisaic circles wrote the *Psalms of Solomon* and the
Testament of Solomon, in which they interpreted the eschatological Son of David as having the divine wisdom of Solomon, and
attributed to him lordship over all demonic forces that controvert-
ed the will of YHWH (*Testament of Solomon,* 3:4 and 15:3). Every
demon was portrayed as knowing and fearing the name of Solomon, Son of David. Psalm 72, designated in our canon as a Psalm
of Solomon, expresses this Solomonic image of the true king who
will bring peace to all the earth:

> Give the king thy justice, O God,
>   and thy righteousness to the royal son! . . .
> In his days may righteousness flourish,
>   and peace abound, till the moon be no more! . . .
> May his name endure for ever,
>   his fame continue as long as the sun!
> May men bless themselves by him,
>   all nations call him blessed!
>
>   Psalm 72:1, 7, 17

This form of the Jewish faith connected the title Son of David
with wisdom, justice, and peace. By the power of God's Spirit, the
Solomonic Son of David exorcizes the demonic from both persons
and society. This attribution of power over the demonic indicates
the apocalyptic sense of history included within this view. History
was seen as a battleground between good and evil powers, and
therefore everything finally depended upon whether the power
exercised in history was the *pneuma* (spirit) of YHWH or of
Beelzebub. The true Son of David shares both God's wisdom and
power in his authority over demons. But there is also the reality
of demonic power, so it was considered essential to "test the spirits," to discern whether divine or demonic power was at work.

This form of the Jewish tradition also was related to Deutero-
Isaiah's vision of the anointed suffering servant in the apocalyptic
literature of this period (cf. *Jubilee* 31:15 and the *Testament of Levi*
18:1, 3). Because the prophet-messiah, God's "servant" and "son,"

is rejected and sent to a martyr's death by his opponents, only the end of history will finally prove his eschatological authority. The *Book of Wisdom* taught that this wise One would enter into his kingship only through suffering (2:19). But in the "last end of the righteous" (2:16), the righteous and wise One will be vindicated (5:1 and 18:3).

This Solomonic Son of David tradition was a clear alternative in Jesus' era to the political messianism of the royal Son of David tradition that inspired the Zealots and Sicarri, but it was nonetheless equally and completely Jewish. To interpret the messiah as a nonviolent latter-day savior figure was not a Christian invention, but clearly an adaptation of an apocalyptic Jewish perspective in first-century Judaism.

Jesus as Eschatological Prophet and Solomonic Son of David

All four canonical Gospels carry the memory that Jesus was first identified as this eschatological messianic prophet, interpreted as the Solomonic Son of David, who both announced and manifested in his ministry the final kingdom of God. This earliest understanding of Jesus provided the bridge between the impact that Jesus made on his disciples during his earthly ministry and the developing Christology of the church's kerygma after his death and resurrection. The principal titles of this later kerygma—Christ, Lord, Son of God—were already to be found in the Jewish intertestamental literature depicting their expected eschatological prophet-messiah. The use New Testament authors made of Hebrew scripture to interpret the eschatological meaning of Jesus was no different from the charismatic hermeneusis widely practiced in the Judaism of their time. The New Testament authors stood within a widely used Jewish hermeneutic that adapted Moses, Elijah, and Enoch, among others, as literary figures to interpret their eschatological hopes in contemporary history.

The momentous difference of the first Christians from this Jewish hermeneusis was their use of this tradition to interpret the actual life of one who had only recently died. What was only a literary device for their Jewish contemporaries became for them a theological basis for a Christ movement responding to Jesus' actual life, death, and resurrection.

The decision of this Christian movement to interpret Jesus with the images and ideas of the tradition expecting an eschatological prophet-messiah shows that Jesus had left no impression or memory of being a messianic freedom fighter. Jesus was received and interpreted as the messenger and prophet of a deeper liberation and a more universal peace. It was and is this Jesus of Nazareth, so remembered and interpreted, who is the norm and criterion of Christian belief in the universal creator God. As such, however, he was not defined against "the" Jewish messianic expectation, but was identified and interpreted by the most adequate Jewish messianic model of the several extant in his era.

It is true, nevertheless, that the New Testament remembered and interpreted Jesus in a way that stretches and stresses the universal meaning of the eschatological prophet-messiah. When this image was appropriated by Jesus in his sermon in the synagogue of Nazareth (Luke 4:14–30), the promise of Isaiah 61:1–2 was reinterpreted so universalistically that his Jewish neighbors were remembered as seeking to throw him from the brow of the hill on which Nazareth is built. The oracle as it continues in Isaiah 61:5–7 promised the Jewish exiles recompense and even retribution for what they had suffered: Aliens would feed their flocks and foreigners become their plowmen; in recompense for their shame, they should have a double portion of the wealth of other nations. Jesus was remembered, and resisted by them, as having told entirely contrasting stories out of their prophetic traditions of Elijah and Elisha—of God acting through Elijah to bring blessing to a Sidonese widow, and through Elisha to bring healing to a Syrian leper.

Those like his Nazareth neighbors who took Jesus only as "Joseph's son" (Luke 4:22; cf. Mark 6:3 and John 6:42), as just a human being like all the rest, are judged in the New Testament as not having understood him. The New Testament faith is clear that Jesus *is* the eschatological prophet-messiah and, as such, God's Son, and to reject him is to reject the One whom God has sent. Those who experienced Jesus' power could not respond to him as though he were just another human being. The joy of Jesus' being and the healing and transforming power of his message were too great for that. According to the New Testament, even some of Jesus' friends thought he was "beside himself" (Mark 3:21), and others who exercised religious and political authority struggled with the decision as to whether Jesus' power was from the Spirit of God or from Satan. Some of these Jerusalem authorities concluded, "He is possessed by Beelzebub, and by the prince of demons he casts out demons" (Mark 3:22). The Synoptic evangelists refute this judgment as self-contradictory, for demonic power could not be used against the demonic (Mark 3:22–27; Matt. 12:24–29; Luke 11:15–22), and then more strongly charge with blasphemy those who would speak of the Holy Spirit expressed through Jesus as demonic (Mark 3:28–30 and Matt. 12:31–32). The first Christian communities held Jesus' power to heal and transform to be that of the eschatological prophet-messiah anointed by the Holy Spirit, interpreted as the Solomonic Son of David.

The Gracious Nature of Jesus' Power

The holiness of Jesus' spirit was to be seen in the nature of his power. Jesus healed and exorcised only to meet the needs of those in dire distress, never to bring advantage to himself or only his own people, nor even to demonstrate or verify that his spirit is the *pneuma* of God. From the temptation narratives at the beginning of his ministry through his refusal, reported in every Gospel, to "give a sign" to his evil generation, unto the very end in his crucifixion, Jesus refused to do legitimating miracles. He used God's power as God's servant only in the service of God's creation. Thus the nature of God's power could be discerned in Jesus by the form of his love. The legitimation of such power is God's alone, perhaps to be proven only at the end when history reaches its fulfillment; or to become known penultimately in the resurrection, as the Christian community came to experience it and finally understand.

It is this quality of power and this alone that is divine. The presence and expression of this power is the reign of God on earth. This power expressed in and through Jesus was the basis for his affirmation that "the kingdom of God has come upon you" (Luke 11:20 and Matt. 12:28). And it is the nature of this power that creates peace. For it hungers and thirsts for righteousness and invests itself at every point to create justice, whether it be the rich man distributing his wealth to the poor, the tax collector restoring fourfold to those whom he extorted, the restoration of the dignity of women who were objects of lust and discrimination, or the "half-breed" Samaritan being honored as the paradigm of neighborliness.

The power of this loving hunger for righteousness creates peace because it is founded on God's righteousness and not its own; thus it seeks God's justice, not its own judgments of others. It is merciful, thus ready to forgive, not once but without limit—seventy times seven. It is meek and thus free from self-assertion, because its self-affirmation is grounded in God's love, known as Jesus' Abba who may become the Abba of all who respond to his love.

This just, merciful, and meek love empowers those who may be genuinely called the "sons of God" because they are "peacemakers." And they remain peacemakers even when they are reviled and persecuted for being so. Their response is to mourn for the peacelessness of the persecutors:

> O Jerusalem, Jerusalem, killing the prophets and stoning those who are sent to you! How often would I have gathered your children together as a hen gathers her brood under her wings, and you would not! Behold, your house is forsaken and desolate.
>
> Matthew 23:37–38; Luke 13:34–35

The Jewish nationalism of Jesus' era, exacerbated by centuries of suffering under Assyrian, Babylonian, Greek, and Roman overlords, had made it difficult for all, and perhaps impossible for some, to recognize this eschatological prophet-messiah, whom other aspects of their own religious tradition had led them to expect. This same religious tradition, however, enabled others to begin to identify the divine meaning of the impact Jesus had upon them while he still lived among them. It provided the symbols and ideas that allowed them to begin to thematize his ultimate significance for the peace of God's whole creation. Before this christological process was completed in the ecumenical councils of the church, it would be recognized that Jesus was much "more than a prophet," as even the later stages of the New Testament kerygma affirmed. But the christological concepts affirmed by the later church were largely developed from symbols related, as we have seen, to the Jewish articulation of the eschatological prophet-messiah they expected, elaborated through the image of the Solomonic Son of David.

The Jewish Form of Faith in the Rejected and Crucified Christ

The Jewish man Jesus was thus discerned to be what Jewish faith had prepared his first Jewish disciples to expect and finally to see. Despite the ideological strains of Jewish nationalism alienated by a long history of suffering, precisely the kind of Jew Jesus was came to be recognized as the prophet-messiah Jews expected. These ideological strains made aspects of the witness of those who did receive and recognize Jesus inadequate to his universal meaning. Indeed, from the vantage of almost two millennia of Christian history, it is now possible to perceive the ideological elements of ecclesial self-interest that made some of their witness a basis for a later terrible anti-Semitism, when non-Jewish nations ideologically misused what in the New Testament is essentially an intra-Jewish critique.

A courageous biblical and ecclesial criticism has enabled much of the church to repent of and finally repudiate that distortion of its gospel.[10] Condemnation of the Jewish faith and Jewish people is not an authentic part of the Christian gospel of universal peace. Although ideological criticism of Jewish ideology and undue Jewish nationalism may properly remain a part of Christian theology's universal critique of the ideological nationalism still found in many nations,[11] our Christian faith in Jesus as the Christ is still a Jewish form of faith in a fully Jewish man.

Anti-Semitic ideology infected Christology especially at the point of trying to understand the repudiation and crucifixion of Jesus. How is it possible that one who so purely and powerfully expressed the Spirit of God could be so utterly and terribly rejected by some of those whose religious experience and longing had led them to expect just such a one as he? But Christian history and experience has since taught the church to recognize the universal and ongoing nature of this rejection, even among us who have long been instructed by a quite orthodox Christology. Thus we must turn in the next chapter to seek to understand how a constantly crucified Jesus is the Christ who gives us God's peace.

3

The Crucifixion of Jesus
and the Dialectic of Peace

Faith in Jesus as the Christ either begins or ends at the fact of his crucifixion. Everything depends on whether, and how, we may answer the question as to why one whose life reflected an utter confidence in the creator God as his Abba, and who lived out his message that God was graciously acting to bring creation to completion, could be so cruelly repudiated and violently destroyed. Either he was wrong about God and thus Christians are wrong about him, or this is the way God's creative power must finally be expressed in a finitely free and often deeply alienated world.

If we dare to conclude that this is the way God's creative power brings the creation to completion in peace, then it becomes possible only to have a highly dialectical view of peace. Any less dialectical view, like Augustine's concept of "the tranquility of order," falters before the image of Jesus' agony in Gethsemane and his cry of dereliction from the cross. If these dimensions of his suffering are allowed to inform our theology, the polarities of gracious action and tragic suffering, spiritual tranquility and social struggle, will be incorporated into our understanding of peace. This dialectical view of peace becomes sufficiently complex and mysterious that even the more rationalistic may accept the New Testament claim that God's peace "passes all human understanding" and that Christ's gift of peace is "not as the world gives." And having faced this mystery, perhaps the mystery of the unity of the human and divine in Jesus may also be illumined for us.

Jesus' Galilean Ministry and Nondialectical Peace

It is possible to infer a less dialectical view of peace from the character of Jesus' earlier Galilean ministry. Although form criticism is convincing that it is impossible to derive a historical reconstruction of Jesus' ministry from the Gospels' accounts of his life and teaching, there is no reason to doubt that they are constructed out of authentic memories of Jesus' actual life and message. And the Gospels present us with a fundamental change from the earlier Galilean proclamation of Jesus, before growing misunderstanding and rejection of his message led him to turn to the preparation of a more intimate group of disciples and to the culmination of his ministry in Jerusalem. Jesus' earliest proclamation was of the nearness of God's gracious reign. He taught that YHWH, his Abba, is moving to transform humanity's history of suffering. The purpose of history, as the end will show, is total satisfaction, joy, peace, the *shalom* of God. God is creative love for all persons, so the poor and hungry and sorrowing may take hope. It is God's "good pleasure" to give humanity the "kingdom" of God's fulfilled creation. Jesus marvelously helps and heals and feeds those who have faith in him.

The whole of this early ministry was characterized with the image of a wedding feast. Quite in contrast to the fasting of the Pharisees and the disciples of John the Baptist, the disciples of Jesus behaved with him as though they were at a feast. Jesus' reply when he was asked about it was, "Can the wedding guests fast while the bridegroom is with them?" (Mark 2:19). The point is that Jesus' presence and action among them were felt and received as the direct offer of God's salvation: love, joy, and peace. Such a presence is festal and must be celebrated.

The most exasperating part of this whole style of behavior, to those who did not believe that this was what was happening, was Jesus' sharing his meals with "sinners." Such table fellowship was forbidden among Jews. Jesus' response was that the invitation to enter again into communion and communication must be carried precisely and especially to sinners. And he dared to confirm his invitation by forgiving their sins (cf. Mark 2:17). His word to the "sinner" who came to him at table in Simon the Pharisee's house was, "Your sins are forgiven. . . . Your faith has saved you; go in peace" (Luke 7:48, 50). Here, indeed, was a direct, nondialectical offer of peace.

The response of the orthodox, however, was to begin "to say among themselves, 'Who is this who even forgives sins?' " (Luke 7:49). In Judaism, as for many others who understand that the justice of the universe is at stake (e.g., Anselm), God alone can forgive sins. To assume such authority for oneself or to ascribe it to another human being is blasphemy. God alone, and that at the end of the age, shall judge. Jesus, as God's eschatological prophet-messiah, however, confirmed his message of the near approach of God's gracious reign by offering sinners God's invitation to his great eschatological feast of fellowship (cf. Matt. 22:1–14 and Luke 14:16–24). Some responded gladly, but many were not ready to presume that God's invitation to the fulfillment of life could be opened so widely and indiscriminately to those who did not share the religious discipline they found necessary to prepare for such ultimate blessing.

The Jerusalem Ministry and Dialectical Peace

Because of growing opposition, Jesus ended his Galilean ministry, perhaps with a sense of failure, and determined—"set his face" (Luke 9:51)—to go to Jerusalem. Almost the whole of the Gospel of Mark, and most of the other Gospels, portray this final period of his ministry as a journey toward suffering and death. Whatever Jesus' own consciousness was, and we cannot reconstruct that historically, the drama of his life now moved to the stage where he must have known the jeopardy in which this move to "official Jerusalem" placed him. Herod Antipas had already beheaded the other prophet, John the Baptist; the Sanhedrin had the authority to stone to death Jews they considered blasphemous; and the Roman procurator had often enough used his power of crucifixion to protect the sovereignty of Rome against rebellious Jews. Though the nature of Jesus' proclamation and ministry was far from the royal messianism that inspired zealotry, Jesus' disciples clearly included former Zealots—at least Simon, "the Zealot" (Luke 6:15), probably Judas Iscariot *(sicarius)*, and perhaps James and John (sons of thunder, *Boanerges*). There was reason to fear the worst, and Jesus and his disciples need not be thought so naïve as not to have been aware of the danger.

Jesus' utter confidence in the gracious power of God to bring his creation to completion, to "give his kingdom" to all who would faithfully receive it, must have required him to integrate not only the possibility of death but the actual threat of his violent death, into his confidence in, and readiness to serve, such an Abba. Even though the record we have of his "passion" is formed by his disciples' post-Easter experiences, their recognition of the crucified Jesus in the resurrected Christ reveals a personal-ontological continuity between their memory of who he was as he went toward his death and his exalted being as the resurrected Christ. There is no attempt in the Gospels to disguise how starkly traumatic an experience this was—they "all forsook him, and fled"—and not only for the disciples but also for Jesus; witness his spiritual agony in the Garden of Gethsemane and on the cross. They remembered him, however, as trying to prepare them for his death.

What clearly they were unprepared for was to accept it, or to understand it, as part of the good news he had been proclaiming of the gracious power of God as the ground of hope for everyone without exception, including the poor, the oppressed, and the sinner. In the idiom of our discussion, they were not ready to move from understanding Christ's offer of peace, as direct, to what we have called a dialectical understanding of peace. The mystery of a peace whose coming includes struggle, rejection, and death was too much for them, as it has proved to be too much for many of us ever since. There is precious little "tranquility" in it, and all too much disorder.

Contemporary Responses to the Dialectic of Peace

The contemporary philosophical theologian Paul Ricoeur has named this difficulty of recognizing the dialectical character of peace—which often amounts to rejecting it—as "an ideological screen of conciliation at any price."[1] Christian faith's belief in peace becomes an ideology justifying rejection of any and all conflict that the struggle for peace in an alienated and unjust world may require. Established forms of ordered disorder are accepted, perhaps even sacralized, by rejecting as unspiritual anything that threatens the precarious peace our world now maintains, or the "inner peace" we sustain by abstracting ourselves from its struggles. If we cannot have peace directly, then often we do not genuinely want it at all. To join peacemaking with persecution for righteousness' sake, as Jesus did in the Beatitudes (Matt. 5:9–10), is not an understanding most human beings can easily share. He may have come to understand this as the way to "the kingdom of heaven" from his reading of the history of persecution of Israel's prophets (Matt. 5:11), but many others prefer a more immediate and direct peace. If we cannot have the "tranquility of order," then we shall accept the tranquility of established disorder.

There are other current-day Christians, however, whose personal and social histories of suffering have opened them to a more dialectical understanding of peace. The German theologian Jürgen Moltmann described his generation of students beginning the study of theology in 1948 in a society shattered by World War II as just such persons:

> Shattered and broken, the survivors of my generation were then returning from camps and hospitals to the lecture room. A theology which did not speak of God in the sight of the one who was abandoned and crucified would have had nothing to say to us then.[2]

It is experiencing full force this "shattered and broken" world, whether in the modern actuality of much innocent suffering in total war and Jewish Holocaust or in the past actuality of the unjust crucifixion of one who loved God's whole creation with a pure heart, that we are driven toward a more dialectical understanding of universal peace—or perhaps to despair of peace altogether. Such despair of universal peace may take many forms, ranging from aggressive self- and group defense in so dangerous a world to passive resignation, perhaps in the religious form of the abstracted spirituality of pure souls who live above the struggle of this evil world.

Personal Sanctification Based on a
Nondialectical Theology of Providence

A dialectical understanding of peace, which remains confident of God's gift of universal peace while remaining engaged in the struggle to realize it in an alienated and conflicted world, requires a more dialectical understanding of God's providential guidance and "governance" of the world. A careful understanding of the concept of governance is especially important. For those who derive their concept of God's power and governance from too close an analogy to the power of political kings and emperors, God's "absolute" power is understood as grounding the established social, political, and economic structures within which we must live out our days and find whatever peace we can. If the "kingdom" Jesus announced is understood to be based on this kind of royal power—King David's kind—then all that exists or occurs must somehow be the expression of God's will. The result is a kind of theological "positivism," in the sense that all that is, simply because it is, must be received positively as the direct actualization of God's intention.

Jesus' ministry, however, implied the rejection of the notion of God's power underlying this concept of governance, in his repudiation of the royal Davidic messianism prevalent in the eschatological expectations of his day. God's power is not, and is not to be, expressed in the creation through this kind of messiah. Nevertheless, the power of cultural inertia in our experience of "sovereign" national and imperial power has continued to distort ideologically our Christian conceptions of the power and governance of God in creation.[3] Thus we try to conceive and live out a nondialectical peace on the basis of God's supposed direct, absolute, provident governance of creation.

This is not to say that no genuine personal/social peace has been sought, and perhaps partly achieved, on the basis of this kind of theology. When it really is believed that the social context for our personal activity is directly grounded in God's creative power, then all of our human action may seek to express quite simply and directly the gracious spirit of joy, reconciliation, and peace that Jesus taught and embodied in his life. The concern for sanctifying all of life—"perfect sanctification"—that has nurtured the spirits of millions in my Wesleyan tradition is clear testimony to the power of this faith. In this tradition, and others like it, Christians are taught that all of the personal and social negativities we experience in life are due to personal sin. The way then to salvation and peace is through personal repentance and transformation. The salvation John Wesley proclaimed for our "original sin" in his sermon of that title was expressed in this highly personal way:

> By repentance and lowliness of heart, the deadly disease of pride is healed; that of self-will by resignation, a meek and thankful submission to the will of God; and for the love of the world in all its branches, the love of God is the sovereign remedy.... Ye know that the great end of religion is to renew our hearts in the image of God, to repair that total loss of righteousness and true holiness which we sustained by the sin of our first parents.[4]

Many Wesleyans have been deeply energized to sanctify themselves in God's creation by this message. As long as the cultural and political histories of Great Britain and the United States could be interpreted within a positive perspective of God's direct governance, this Wesleyan form of sanctification could guide an effective Christian praxis of peace.

Relative Dualism, Dialectical Providence, and Social Transformation

What is excised from this positive notion of providence, however, is the experience of the power of the demonic that was so prevalent in the more apocalyptic consciousness and religion of Jesus' era, as we have seen in chapter 2. All of Judaism and Christianity, of course, finally rejected any ultimate dualism that conceives of a Satanic power equivalent to the creator God. For all monotheistic theology, only God is the source of all being. Finite being may become alienated from, and rebellious against, God; but there is no purely evil source of being that stands ultimately over against God. The Judaeo-Christian myth and doctrine of creation rejects all such dualistic ontology. Within this monotheistic affirmation of being, however, many have also affirmed the reality and power of the "demonic."

This idea entered Hebrew theology during the experience of the Exile, perhaps under the influence of Persian Zoroastrian dualism. Despite the Hebrew prophetic interpretation of their exile(s) as YHWH's punishment for their sinful violation of covenant with God, not all aspects of Assyrian, Babylonian, or Persian power

could be understood as mediating God's power. Cyrus, the Persian
emperor who freed the exiles to return home, might be received as
one of God's "messiahs," whose power derived from YHWH's
"anointing" (Isa. 45:1), but certainly not every act of Nebuchad-
nezzar and Sennacherib could be so interpreted. The agonized
response in many Jewish souls reflects their sense of the demonic
in this foreign imperial power. Psalm 137 expresses powerfully this
sense of the demonic, as well as the spiritual distortion in seeking
an equally demonic vengeance:

> By the water of Babylon,
>   there we sat down and wept,
>   when we remembered Zion. . . .
> O daughter of Babylon, you devastator!
>   Happy shall he be who requites you
>   with what you have done to us!
> Happy shall he be who takes your little ones
>   and dashes them against the rock!
> Psalm 137:1, 8–9

Jewish suffering under the subsequent Greek and Roman imperi-
ums only served to increase this sense of the demonic, as the
apocalyptic expressions of faith in the century in which Jesus lived
clearly show.

Jewish and Christian apocalyptic contains what may be designated only as a "relative dualism." It is relative in the sense that
the *creatio ex nihilo* that expresses and safeguards Judaeo-Christian monotheism from any form of ontological dualism is affirmed;
and dualistic in the sense that sin is understood as not only personal
but as demonic structures of evil that stand against God's purposes
for creation. Paul Tillich reintroduced this concept of the demonic
into modern Protestant theology in 1926 to interpret the conflicted
reality of Europe after World War I. Consistent with Judaeo-
Christian relative dualism, he interpreted demonic structures as
resting upon God's creative power, as all creation must, but as
having so distorted God's creation over so long a period of history
that they have become powerful historic forces of bondage and
destruction. Demonic structures dialectically unite forces of creativity and destruction, meaning and meaninglessness.[5] Prepared
with this concept, Tillich was ready to name Nazism as properly

"demonic" when it emerged in his national history, and to struggle against its idolatrous nationalism and racism toward a more universal peace.

Christian theology in North America, however, was by and large not ready to accept this category as Tillich moved to the United States as a refugee in 1933. An undialectical theology of God's positive providence continued in American spirituality, correlated with what the American church historian Timothy Smith has described as the "optimism of a new nation, where hopes were blooming for a social order hallowed by divine grace and hence characterized by justice and love."[6] American theology in the Wesleyan mode I know best had recovered from Wesley's own rejection of the American Revolution as "anarchistic."[7] American Wesleyans interpreted the Revolution within the direct providence of God and sent a delegation from the founding Christmas Conference of 1784 to assure President Washington of their loyal support. If either had had a more dialectical understanding of peace, which recognized the demonic dimension of all violence resulting from competing economic and political structures, they might have recognized the ambiguity of the Revolution and considered that in some ways both Wesley and his American followers were right and wrong.

The British Methodist theologian Rupert Davies has articulated the basis in Wesley's theology for both his rejection of the American Revolution and the American Wesleyans' assurance that they continued to stand in the direct providence of God:

> Wesley's holiness was social in the narrow sense that it related to personal relations with other people. . . . It is wholly fair to say that he thought of Scriptural holiness as being practiced *within the existing order.* Nor does his belief that Christian perfection is possible in this life really supply a bridge to the belief that society can and should be transformed within the present historical context.[8]

The British ideological strain in Wesley's own thought resisted any acceptance of so radical a struggle for social transformation as the American Revolution within his view of God's positive providence, while the ideological vector in American Wesleyans' thought led them to see the Revolution as part and parcel of God's direct

providence in their life. The difference in perspective is traceable
to where each stood in relation to the "existing order." Neither
took seriously, however, the theological possibility of a more dialectical understanding of God's providential relation to established
order/disorder, because they did not take seriously the reality of
demonic structures in their history.

Contemporary American Spirituality and the Dialectic of Peace

To the degree that American spirituality and theology has remained at home in the existing order as God's providential order,
it was ill-prepared to deal with the "time of troubles" into which
the United States entered after World War II. The "liberalism"
that expressed America's utopian millennial expectations that the
achievement of national peace based on liberty and justice for all
would lead the whole world toward a universal peace based on
freedom and democracy has given way to a "conservatism" that
now looks to America's economic and military force to impose
stability on a dangerously disordered world, threatened by the
growing influence of a demonic "evil empire."

The nuclear arms race, the Vietnam war, and the national civil
rights struggle of its black minority have been enough to convince
some American Christians, but far from all, that they must take
a more dialectical view of God's providential relation to national
structures that exhibit such demonic dimensions. This shift in
theological perspective, however, is strenuously opposed by the
"civil religion" articulated by America's political leaders. Even
after America's ulcer burst in 1968 as a consequence of the black
civil rights struggle and the anti-Vietnam war movement, and in
the midst of his own "Watergate," President Richard Nixon could
say in his second inaugural address in 1973:

> Above all else, the time has come for us to renew our faith
> in ourselves and in America. In recent years that faith has
> been severely challenged. . . . America's record in this cen-
> tury has been unparalleled in the world's history for its re-
> sponsibility, for its generosity, for its creativity, and for its
> progress.[9]

One might add that, to the degree Mr. Nixon's judgment was true,
it is a sad commentary on the world's history. After more than a

decade, the far greater rhetorical gifts of Ronald Reagan, however, have finally reestablished for many their faith in America as standing directly in God's providence. Thus the exercise of American force can be equated with God's power, and any recognition of demonic evil is dualistically and nondialectically attributed to the "evil empire" of the Soviet Union.

In this perspective, the biblical promise of and hope for universal peace, mediated through the mercy and grace that entered our history in Jesus, is repudiated as liberal utopianism. The struggle to overcome enmity through love of the enemy gives way to an apocalyptic zealotry that is ready to submit the world to nuclear war so that the messianic age might come. Christians are called literally to arms, and perhaps to Armageddon. Grace, mercy, and peace are, if not forgotten, at least reduced to a purely personal realm and socially postponed until a Kingdom that God will give beyond the history we now know.

So in fact the commitment to sanctification, in the kind of theological formation that theologians like John Wesley gave it, has had a hard time surviving after a society enters such a time of troubles. Professor John Kent's sociological critique of British Methodism, which led him to the judgment that Wesley's "myth of the holy life . . . did not usefully survive the collapse of the *ancien régime*,"[10] seems to be as true for the United States following World War II as it was for Great Britain after World War I. Once the positive view of providence on which it was based was deeply shaken, few Christians could any longer genuinely practice so limited a form of personal sanctification, unless they remained captive to their national ideology.

Christ's Crucifixion, Dialectical Panentheism, and Universal Peace

Professor Moltmann, as already noted, took up the study of theology after World War II with a spirit deeply chastened by the destruction of two world wars and the utter bankruptcy of his German national ideology. After decades of reflection on what he had learned, he published his Christology under the provocative title *The Crucified God.* He turned so far away from any notion of God's sovereign power as the direct providential source of all

events as to affirm that God himself suffers. Though he skirted the
ancient "heresy" of patripassionism by affirming the trinitarian
distinctions between Father and Son, he nevertheless posited suffering in both persons of the Trinity as Jesus went to the cross:
"The Son suffers in his love being forsaken by the Father as he dies.
The Father suffers in his love the grief of the death of the Son."[11]
Professor Moltmann suggested by this formulation that God's relational, trinitarian being is opened by the suffering of Jesus to all the
suffering of the world:

> The "bifurcation" in God must contain the whole uproar of
> history within itself. Men must be able to recognize rejection,
> the curse, and final nothingness in it. The cross stands be-
> tween the Father and the Son in all the harshness of its
> forsakenness. . . . All human history, however much it may
> be determined by guilt and death, is taken up into this "his-
> tory of God," i.e., into the Trinity, and integrated into the
> future of the "history of God." There is no suffering which
> in this history of God is not God's suffering, no death which
> has not been God's death in the history on Golgotha. There-
> fore, there is no life, no fortune, and no joy which have not
> been integrated by his history into eternal life, the eternal joy
> of God. To think of "God in history" always leads to theism
> and to atheism. To think of "history in God" leads beyond
> that into new creation and *theopoiesis.*[12]

Moltmann uses the concept of "panentheism" to point beyond
the "theism" of positive providence and the "atheism" that denies
God any providential relation to history because of the demonic
reality of evil in it. Panentheism is not an abstract concept for
Moltmann, because he sees it as expressing the peculiar experience
of communion with Christ:

> Life in communion with Christ is full life in the trinitarian
> situation of God. Dead in Christ and raised to new life, as
> Paul said in Romans 6:8, the believer really participates in
> the suffering of God in the world, because he partakes in the
> suffering of the love of God. Conversely, he takes part in the
> particular suffering of the world, because God has made it his
> suffering in the cross of his Son. . . . Therefore in communion
> with Christ, it can truly be said . . . "that they live, move, and
> have their being in God" (Acts 17:28). Understood in pan-

theistic terms, that would be a dream which would have to ignore the negative element in the world. But a trinitarian theology of the cross perceives God in the negative element and therefore the negative element in God, and in this *dialectical way is panentheistic.* [13]

The concept "panentheism" is a shorthand way of saying "all is *in* God," as distinguished from "all is God." To speak of "dialectical" panentheism is to affirm that the demonic we experience in history is taken into God and transformed. To use "dialectical panentheism" as a way of understanding the Trinity is to say that the suffering and death of Jesus on the cross is the event that opens the very heart of God, the eternal relation of the Father and the Son, to the historical suffering of a fallen creation. Those dimensions of the world fallen into demonic bondage are returned to participation in the being of God and thus to transformation through the power of God's suffering love. Moltmann describes this in terms of the religious experience of Christian faith:

> He is in fact taken up into the inner life of God, if in the cross of Christ he experiences the love of God for the godless, the enemies, in so far as the history of Christ is the inner life of God himself. In that case, if he lives in this love, he lives in God and God in him. . . . By the secular cross on Golgotha, understood as open vulnerability and as the love of God for loveless and unloved, dehumanized men, God's being and God's life is open to true man. [14]

I have quoted Moltmann at such length because I think his concept of dialectical panentheism enables a conceptual grasp of the meaning of the crucifixion that helps us move beyond the undialectical notion of peace correlated with a positive providence, which some derive from the Galilean portion of Jesus' ministry, to the dialectical understanding of peace and providence that may be correlated with the horror and the meaning of Jesus' crucifixion. We need not agree with every aspect of this formulation to appreciate the brilliance of this concept to illumine a more adequate understanding of how God through Christ transforms a demonic history toward universal peace. Indeed, in chapter 5, where we consider more carefully the trinitarian concept of Logos, some critical disagreement will be indicated. For now, however, it is more important to focus on its illumination.

This illumination is crucial because the history of the church's ministry—and failure in ministry—for universal peace convinces me that Professor Moltmann was correct when he concluded, "Whether or not Christianity, in an alienated, divided, and oppressive society, itself becomes alienated, divided, and an accomplice of oppression, is ultimately decided only by whether the crucified Christ is a stranger to it or the Lord who determines the form of its existence."[15] Jesus' original disciples at first found the crucified Christ a stranger. The evidence of the Gospels is clear, and even overwhelming, that they disguised their relation to him, denied their earlier faith in him, and fled the scene of his crucifixion for the relative safety of home.[16] The reaction of many contemporary Christians is all too similar when existentially having to face the stark reality of the demonic history that crucified him. When that context finally forces us to face what Jesus meant when he asked his first disciples to "take up their cross and follow him," Christians all too often prefer to take up their weapons, even today their thermonuclear weapons, or to retire from the struggle entirely for some spiritual or social haven.

Communion with the Crucified Christ as the Basis for Peace

It was, of course, the experience of Jesus' resurrection that transformed the meaning of the cross for his first disciples, to which I shall turn in the next chapter. Apart from the resurrection, there would have been no theological recognition that Jesus' crucifixion must finally be understood as an event in the trinitarian being of God. But there was a crucial event before the crucifixion that provided the basis for their recognition of Jesus in his resurrected form, to which we must first turn.

Jesus' eating of the "last supper" with his disciples sought to, and finally did, provide them with an assurance of salvation and peace when face to face with the demonic and death. It allowed them to understand that "he died just as he lived, and he lived as he died."[17] Although the accounts we have in the Gospels are formed by the eucharistic observances they had learned to practice after his resurrection, there is a strong core of historical memory at their base. We have already noted that, in his Galilean ministry, Jesus often enacted the offer of God's salvation through a shared meal of fellowship. Just before his arrest, Jesus offered his most intimate disciples one last sign of God's continuing offer of salvation, in the very jaws of the demonic event he was about to suffer.

There were two crucial elements in this last fellowship meal that Jesus hosted for his intimate friends: (1) the emphatic announcement of his imminent death—this meal is a farewell to their earthly fellowship; and (2) the promise of their fellowship to be renewed in the coming reign of God—"Truly I say to you, I shall not drink again of the fruit of the vine until that day when I drink it new in the kingdom of God" (Mark 14:25). The latter half of this remembered saying may be conditioned by the form of faith following the resurrection, but the bedrock historical fact is that, in the face of his death, Jesus continued to offer his disciples what had become the symbol for them of his message of God's action for their salvation. Despite the rejection he and they had experienced, and the demonic death he faced, Jesus continued to act with full assurance that God was offering his salvation through him. His obedient participation in God's action would continue, no matter how demonic the historical context, in full confidence that God's kingdom was being given and would be given.

It was precisely this memory that kept the experience of resurrection, when it occurred, from becoming a basis for turning to a purely triumphalistic and transcendent experience of mystical salvation above or beyond the demonic struggles of history, and kept the disciples from interpreting the resurrected Christ as finally the revelation of the sovereign power of a royal Davidic messiah that Jesus had repudiated during his earthly ministry. The resurrected Christ was recognized as the crucified Jesus, the same Jesus whose entire ministry had to be interpreted in terms of the eschatological prophet-messiah, who was the Son of David only in the Solomonic sapiental sense. He could be interpreted in the early churches, as today, only as the incarnation of the Wisdom/Word/Logos of God, revealing God's universal action to bless his entire creation with the completion in peace that God eternally intends.

Jesus' disciples, following Jesus himself, came to understand Jesus' death as integrated into his total mission, as his ultimate service that the reign of God's grace might come to bring the creation to completion. The demonic forces inherent in Roman imperialism, Jewish nationalism, and human fear, pride, and alienation might bring Jesus to violent death, but they could not destroy the mission and meaning of his whole life as God's offer of peace. Thus there is no unbridgeable gap between the life, message, and death of the historical Jesus, remembered especially in the *anamnesis* of his Last Supper, and the Christ of faith proclaimed by the church following the resurrection. The spiritual continuity that bridges the gap which otherwise might appear is the Christian experience of the Holy Spirit, received especially in the Holy Communion as the very spirit of the eschatological prophet-messiah who had been fully anointed with God's Spirit during his life, and even unto death.

The theology that emerges from being grounded in and participating in Christ's Holy Spirit is finally a trinitarian Christology, which understands the total event of Jesus' life, death, and resurrection as an event in the trinitarian being of God. The relation that Jesus had sustained with his Abba during life, and through death, was now experienced and conceived as the ground for his disciples' participation in the eternal process of God's salvation of the whole creation. As such, it is also the ground of hope for the Christian's continued participation in the dialectic that brings us both personal peace and requires us to struggle for social peace in full recognition of the demonic forces that distort even our lives and our society. For God is in this struggle, and the whole of it is in God, where it is being transformed through gracious forgiveness into new possibility. In such dialectical panentheism we may "rest" both conceptually and existentially, for it is the power of the Holy Spirit that gives us both life and peace.

4

The Resurrection of Christ
and the Spirit of Peace

At the heart of Christian (and not only Christian) religious experience is the experience and affirmation of life: human life, abundant life, holy life, eternal life. To use abstract academic terms like "dialectical panentheism," as I did at the conclusion of the last chapter, tends to obscure this concrete reality, despite their value as summary concepts. Thus I must begin this chapter by using far more concrete terms. We are concerned with power that creates, sustains, and fulfills life, which when we experience and finally identify it must be understood as divine—the power of God.

Human concern for the fulfillment of life, as we have seen, roots in our dialectical experience of both gratefully receiving the gracious gift of life, through biological, familial, and cultural processes, and anxiously suffering the destructive, alienating, and conflicting forces that limit, divide, and destroy life. Concern for life becomes ultimate and religious at the intersection of life and death, where our adoration of the Creator of life becomes the basis for our resolve to struggle against all the forces of destruction and death.

This ultimate concern for life may be focused, as we have, in the symbol of the struggle for peace—which in its full biblical connotation points to the "wholeness" of personal integrity and social communion in all of humanity. This biblical understanding of peace as *shalom,* however, also affirms that such wholeness can be achieved only in covenant relation with God, who, as the universal Creator of all being, embraces the whole and makes it whole. We

human beings, in our finitude, particularity, and various shades of
alienation and despite our affirmation of life and concern for peace,
do not know this wholeness, or even very clearly how to move
toward it. In the midst of life, we are in death—not only the death
we mourn in hospitals and mortuaries but the death we have
caused in Auschwitz and Hiroshima, continue to prepare in Penta-
gon and Kremlin, and confront in our media every day—especially, from the perspective of this study, the conflict between
Palestinian and Jew in what for both them and us is the "holy
land."

It is holy for all Christians because it is the very place where
Jesus of Nazareth graciously announced and expressed the power
of God that brings human life to fulfillment by creating peace. Yet
the peace Jesus brought and brings seems utterly paradoxical to
many, because it was finally accomplished only through the cruel
repudiation and violent destruction he had to suffer. This cruel
paradox is resolved for Christian faith only in the experience of
Jesus' resurrection, in which he remains a living presence in the
midst of our worship and service. What had been a palpable,
physical presence for thirty years in the Holy Land became a
powerful spiritual Presence in every land, capable of bringing life
out of death, peace out of conflict, and wholeness out of particularity.[1]

The Meaning of Jesus' Resurrection from the Dead

It was precisely this experience of Jesus' continued presence after
his violent death that is at the root of Christian faith in his resurrection. The Christian scriptures nowhere provide a description of the
phenomenon of resurrection, though they do describe an empty
tomb (Matt. 28:6; Luke 24:3; John 20:1–10). Yet in every description of the experience of the empty tomb, the authors of the Gospels make clear that this experience was not the basis of their belief.
Not only is the women's report dismissed as an old wives' tale (see
Luke 24:11), but Peter's own inspection of the tomb leaves him
only "wondering" in Luke (24:12) and unbelieving in John (20:6–7
and 9–10, esp. v. 9), while the Jerusalem authorities undertook to
interpret it as grave robbery (Matt. 28:11–15).

What was convincing for the first apostles, and is the bedrock of the faith in Jesus' resurrection, was their "seeing" him as alive after his crucifixion. They understood their seeing, however, as a being given to see—as a vision, or a revelation. This is clearly taught in Luke's account of Jesus' appearance to the two disciples on the way to Emmaus, whose eyes at first "were kept from recognizing him" (24:16), while later they "were opened" so they could recognize him before he vanished out of their sight (24:31). Paul similarly recounts the history of Jesus' appearance to Cephas (Peter), the Twelve, five hundred brethren, James, all the apostles, and finally to himself, in each case as *ophthe*, "was seen" (1 Cor. 15:5–8). This is a way of expressing passive seeing, which is a being given to see—a form for expressing the reception of revelation.

The apostles interpreted the revelation of Jesus alive after death in terms of "resurrection," which was expected by many Jews only at the end of the age as a general resurrection *of* the dead (cf. Dan. 12:2). The spiritual Presence of Jesus interpreted as resurrected *from* the dead was the apostles' way of continuing to express on the other side of Jesus' crucifixion the same eschatological hope he had begun to arouse in them during his life. The gracious creator God, whom Jesus knew as Abba, was present in and through him to give his "kingdom," establish his creative purpose, and bring life to fulfillment. Jesus' life, death, and resurrection as a total event is the beginning of history's new eon. Jesus Christ as "the first-born from the dead" (Col. 1:18) is the sure sign that history's "night is far gone, the day is at hand" (Rom. 13:12).

It is also important to understand that the affirmation of Jesus as "resurrected from the dead" requires the equally clear affirmation that he really died. There is nothing in these scriptural accounts akin to modern mortuary experiences where the cosmetic preparation of the dead allows the illusion that they have not really died. The resurrected Christ the first apostles experienced as spiritual Presence was clearly the crucified Jesus, with scarred hands and feet where cruel nails had fastened him to the cross (John 20:20 and 25–28).

To know the Easter joy of the resurrected Christ only in complete continuity with the suffering and death of the crucified Jesus is crucial for our understanding of the peace that Christ gives. For then we cannot neglect, as the apostles also did not, the message and life-style of Jesus that led to his death. Professor Schillebeeckx has put this point with force and clarity in his monumental study, *Christ: The Experience of Jesus as Lord:*

> The death of Jesus was no coincidence, but the intrinsic historical consequence of the radicalism of both his message and his life-style, which showed that all "master-servant" relationships were incompatible with the life-style of the kingdom of God. The very radicalism of this proclamation as an intrinsic element in a consistent life-style provoked the fatal resistance of others. . . . This radical universality of a will for salvation-for-all, without any exclusiveness, provoked the well-known and equally radical counter-reaction of "this world."[2]

Jesus' message, life-style, death, and resurrection constitute for Christians an integral event of revelation. To receive and participate in it is to experience salvation—to begin again the living process toward personal and social wholeness, integrity, and reconciliation that is genuine peace. The resurrection is not a reversal of the disastrous consequence of Jesus' life but a confirmation of the eternal validity of that life-style. Jesus' paradigm of doing good and resisting evil and suffering, regardless of the immediate historical consequences, has an unconditional validity. Jesus' resurrection is the final dimension of Jesus' revelation of the living God, who is present and active to bring a finite and alienated creation to completion in peace.

The Holy Spirit of Peace

The first Christians experienced the resurrection of Jesus in terms of the gift of peace and their responsibility for peace. John's Gospel is most explicit at this point. The resurrected Jesus' first words to fearful disciples huddled behind locked doors were "Peace be with you" (John 20:20; cf. Luke 24:36); and his second word was to send them to continue his mission of peace: "Jesus said to them again, 'Peace be with you. As the Father has sent me, even so I send you' " (John 20:21). Through the resurrected Christ they knew again personal and interpersonal peace in their intimate circle, and they knew their responsibility to move out of that circle to share Christ's peace with their world, which was now clearly again God's world.

Jesus also spoke and enacted a third word in his resurrection appearances, which has had tremendous existential impact upon all Christians ever since: "And when he had said this, he breathed on them, and said to them, 'Receive the Holy Spirit' " (John 20:22). In the form given to this text, there is clear allusion to the Jewish understanding of God's gift of life in the original creation of human beings: "Then the LORD God formed A-dam of the dust from the ground, and breathed into his nostrils the breath of life; and A-dam became a living being" (Gen. 2:7, modified). Christians received, and have understood themselves ever since as receiving through Christ, the creative Spirit of God that again enables them truly to live. Whatever their personal histories of limitation and failure, however deeply alienated from the springs of life in family and culture, no matter how deeply wounded or possessed by demonic structures, persons may know again through Christ the Holy Spirit that engenders, empowers, and fulfills life.

Such fulfillment clearly requires a going out from self into renewed relation with one's alienated and conflicted world. Jesus' resurrection is completed in both the sending of the Spirit to his disciples and their sending into the world. All other appearances of the risen Jesus reported in the Synoptic Gospels, like that in John, express this sending of the disciples (Mark 16:15; Luke 24:47; Matt. 28:19). Their mission as expressed in the Synoptics was to preach, teach, and baptize; but in John's Gospel it is also clear that this is primarily a mission of reconciliation: "If you forgive the sins of any, they are forgiven; if you retain the sins of any, they are retained" (John 20:23). The gift of the Spirit is for the forgiveness of sins, just as baptism in the Holy Spirit is for the forgiveness of sins, according to John the Baptist's words about Jesus (John 1:29, 33). The sin that had diminished, divided, and destroyed life is to be forgiven, and the demonic structures sin has created and sustained in history are to be overcome. This is the gift and the work of the Holy Spirit. To receive and participate in such a Spirit is the Easter event of participation in Christ's resurrection.

The Holy Spirit is the spirit of peace and reconciliation in the Christian gospel. The gift of such a Spirit is its good news. The sharing of such a Spirit is its mission. Yet it remains difficult for many to understand this when it is expressed in terms of spirit and the Holy Spirit. We may be able to give phenomenological meaning to peace and reconciliation in psychological, social, and political terms at the human level, but how are we to understand the theological meaning of Spirit in relation to our human spirits? This difficulty has been compounded for many of us now that modern psychology, following philosophical idealism, has substituted the term "mind" *(psyche)* for the more apt theological term "spirit" *(pneuma).*

To seek to express the personal center of human sensation, feeling, thought, will, and action only in terms of "mind," as modern thought influenced by the subjectivistic empiricism of Descartes, Locke, and Hume has, is to obscure crucial dimensions of human experience and existence. We are not passionless minds; our personal center is not only logical intellect. As human beings, we are dynamic, rational, deciding persons who are sometimes able to integrate the inorganic, organic, and psychic dimensions of our being in personal actualization and action. In cognitive and moral action, we are sometimes able as centered selves to deliberate and decide in a way that includes and integrates the relevant events in our bodies and environment which impinge on our central nervous systems. It is this free, self-integrating, and self-transcendent action, which at the same time is clearly related to and dependent upon the dynamics of our bodies and our world, that is designated "spirit" at the human level.

The philosophical theologian Paul Tillich has described the "moral act" of the human "spirit" in the following insightful way:

> Here, also, a large amount of material is present in the psychological center—drives, inclinations, desires, more or less compulsory trends, moral experiences, ethical traditions and authorities, relations to other persons, social conditions. But the moral act is not the diagonal in which all these vectors limit each other and converge; it is the centered self which actualizes itself as a personal self by distinguishing, separating, rejecting, preferring, connecting, and in doing so, transcending its elements. The act, or more exactly the whole complex of acts, in which this happens has the character of freedom, not freedom in the bad sense of the indeterminacy of an act of the will, but freedom in the sense of a total reaction of a centered self which deliberates and decides.[3]

Human spirit, then, is understood to be that free and related center of being that rationally and morally integrates the dynamics of life, without repression of its own vitality or alienation from its dynamic interrelatedness with others. Spirit is known at the point of personal integration of dynamics and reason or, put another way, in the "union of power and meaning."⁴ It is the dimensions of dynamics and power that are obscured or lost in reducing "spirit" to the rationality and meaning of "mind." This, in turn, can lead to the loss of the vital feeling of relatedness, which reveals the person's internal relation to society and history. Thus it is crucial both for understanding human life and the meaning of Christian faith to recover the full meaning of "spirit." Indeed, it is only those who know and understand themselves at the level of spirit who can fully enter into the experience of and struggle for peace. For peace is precisely the realization of integrity and wholeness in the integration of both the personal and social dimensions of life. And to understand the human spirit in this way enables us to go on to understand the theological meaning of the Holy Spirit.

The Holy Spirit of the Trinitarian God

The Christian experience of the Holy Spirit is known in the "ecstasy" of our human spirits and was primally known by Christ's disciples in their awe-full and wonderful experiencing of Jesus being alive after his crucifixion. Religious ecstasy in the Easter experience has its usual meaning of "standing outside of oneself" *(ek-stasis):* that is, of having the center of one's self opened by the spiritual impact of something ultimately powerful and sublimely valuable.

The Easter accounts in the Gospels are filled with expressions of such ecstasy. The women at the very beginning of this experience respond with "fear and great joy" (Matt. 28:8), affirmatively expressed in Mark as "trembling and astonishment" (Mark 16:8). When the risen Christ first confronts the apostles, they were "startled and frightened, and supposed that they saw a spirit [*pneuma*]," according to Luke 24:37; but when they are convinced that what they saw is the crucified Jesus wonderfully alive, their experience turns to "joy and wonder" (Luke 24:41). When Thomas at last confronts the risen Jesus so that he ceases being "faithless but believing," his ecstatic response to Jesus of Nazareth is, "My Lord [*Kyrios*] and my God [*Theos*]" (John 20:27–28).

These scriptural expressions are pregnant with theological meaning. The apostles experienced a reality that drove them beyond their usual subjective response to the objective phenomena of their environment. Their spirits were ecstatically opened in astonishment, fear, joy, and wonder. The fright caused by the supposition that they saw a "spirit" indicates the dualism that haunted their hellenistic-Jewish minds and world. They felt and feared that there could be "spirits," dissociated from the natural structures of their existence and experience, which very well might be demonic. This dualistically inspired fear, however, gives way to joy and wonder when they are convinced that this "spirit" remains united with the full person *(hypostasis)* of Jesus. Whatever the form of his "spiritual body" (Paul in 1 Cor. 15:44), this "spirit" is neither experienced nor to be conceived dualistically, for it is precisely the continuing person of Jesus whom they knew so well in Capernaum and Jerusalem. But now they ecstatically respond to him risen as "Lord and God." Their Jewish monotheism is ecstatically broken open to include Jesus as God, or in God. What they had known in his life, and paradoxically in his death, is now fully received and affirmed as divine.

The concept of integrity is crucial to the theological understanding of this scriptural witness. The risen Christ is experienced in the full integrity of the personhood of Jesus; he is not a disassociated or alienated "spirit." Neither does the ecstasy of the apostles' experience undermine or destroy their personal integrity. They are not demonically possessed or divided. Their personal centers are ecstatically opened in adoration and wonder in a way that doesn't undermine, but finally strengthens, their personal resolve. This experience becomes the basis for their renewed personal purpose and communal mission. It doesn't remove them from their world but sends them into it to transform it. Precisely because it grounds and strengthens their human spirits, they affirm what they have received through the risen Christ as the Holy Spirit. This experience integrates the power of their created being with a new integrity that allows them to affirm and move toward universal meaning. They know in the Holy Spirit, which is Jesus Christ's Spirit, the "union of power and meaning" of which Tillich speaks—the ultimate power and universal meaning of the Creator God. Tillich's elucidation of this in philosophical-theological categories is helpful:

> The spirit, a dimension of finite life, is driven into a successful self-transcendence; it is grasped by something ultimate and unconditional. It is still the human spirit; it remains what it is, but at the same time it goes out of itself under the impact of the Divine Spirit. . . . Although the ecstatic character of the experience of Spiritual Presence does not destroy the rational structure of the human spirit, it does something the human spirit could not do by itself. When it grasps man it creates unambiguous life.[5]

"Unambiguous life" is to participate in the divine life of the living God. But what of the integrity of God? This renewed and strengthened human integrity appears to be at the cost of the oneness of God. The integrity of the risen Jesus Christ is now affirmed as divine. He also is "Lord and God." The monotheism so precious to Jewish faith, so tenaciously protected for centuries against the religious polytheism and mythological dualism of their Greco-Roman world, now seems clearly at risk in the renewed faith of these Jewish Christians. Is the integrity of God to be sacrificed to the integrity of their historical existence?

This issue of the integrity of God is precisely what led these Jewish Christians finally toward the insight that God's integrity must be conceived as trinitarian. Although there is no fully developed concept of the Trinity in the New Testament, John, the latest and most theologically reflective of the canonical Gospels, clearly sets the terms for this trinitarian development. John regularly speaks of Jesus as not only "the Son of God" (3:16, 3:18, 5:25, 10:36, and 11:4) but as "the only begotten [*monogenous*] Son of God" (3:16 and 3:18). Whoever else may be called so, Jesus uniquely and only actualizes this divine genus of "Son of God." In Paul's letters, this predicate had first been associated with Jesus' resurrection: He was "designated Son of God in power according to the Spirit of holiness by his resurrection from the dead" (Rom. 1:4). The later Synoptic Gospels associated this affirmation with the event of Jesus' baptism in the Jordan: "A voice came from heaven, 'Thou art my beloved Son; with thee I am well pleased' "

(Mark 1:11 and parallels). All of this Christian confession, however, was directly subsequent to the self-awareness of Jesus himself. He had regularly addressed God in prayer as Abba ("father" in intimate terms), and God as Abba had completely filled Jesus' consciousness (cf. Matt. 11:27; Luke 10:22). Thus, after his death and resurrection, the apostles affirmed Jesus as uniquely the Son of the eternal God whom he had served in life and death unto life again.[6]

The Holy Spirit is similarly posited in the witness of the New Testament. Jesus, who baptized with the Holy Spirit (John 1:33), prepared his disciples for his death by promising them the Holy Spirit as "another paraclete" (John 14:16)—that is, another helper, counselor, and intercessor—who would enable them to continue the work Jesus had begun (John 14:12; 14:26; 15:26–27; 16:7–15). Just as Jesus was their paraclete during his lifetime, so shall they know the Holy Spirit as "another paraclete" after his death and resurrection, when Jesus has returned to be their heavenly "paraclete with the Father" (1 John 2:1).

The New Testament witness, most clearly in the Johannine literature, also associates the Holy Spirit with the gift of peace. The promise of the Holy Spirit as paraclete in John 14:26 is immediately followed with the promise of Christ's peace: "Peace I leave with you; my peace I give to you; not as the world gives do I give to you. Let not your hearts be troubled, neither let them be afraid" (John 14:27). And this spiritual/Spiritual peace is to have clear socioethical expression. The Holy Spirit, the paraclete in our continuing history, and Jesus Christ, our heavenly paraclete, who is the expiation not only for our sins but for those of the "whole world" (1 John 2:2), enables us to participate in God's perfect and universal love for the world (1 John 2:5).

> He who says he is in the light and hates his brother is in the darkness still. He who loves his brother abides in the light.
> 1 John 2:9–10

Just as the Abba who makes his sun rise on the evil and the good is the paradigm for love of enemies in Jesus' remembered teaching (Matt. 5:44–45), so the Holy Spirit of the Son enables human spirits with new and powerful integrity to overcome enmity and reestablish peace through the love of brothers and sisters in the whole world.

The Trinitarian Basis for Dialectical Peace

The sense of spirit developed above sees it as the integrating center of dynamic relationships mediated psychosomatically with its entire world. The hypostasis of a person is precisely such a spiritual center of social relation, constituted by the integrity of his or her self-integration. Such integrity becomes merely formal and empty, however, to the degree that it is cut off from the dynamic relatedness that constitutes it. Modern concepts of experience, which stress the immediacy of subjectivity since Descartes's *cogito ergo sum,* tend toward a subjectivistic narcissism in which the objects of experience become pure object: that is, totally objectified. When this happens, all sense of participatory relation with what is experienced is lost; to the degree it happens, the objective world of nature and society becomes cold, strange, alien, and enemy. This is what "spiritual alienation" means—to be constituted as a finite center of integrated spirit in a way that alienates one from one's world, and perhaps from one's own body, and thus in both cases from the deep dynamics of the self. Martin Buber has written:

> What is decisive is whether the spirit—the You-saying, responding spirit—remains alive and actual; . . . whether what abides of it in individual human life incorporates itself again in communal life. But that certainly cannot be accomplished by dividing communal life into independent realms that also include "the life of the spirit."[7]

The spirit becomes alienated spirit in any individual where the experience of subjectivity constitutes an "independent realm" in which there is little or no sense of internal relation to one's community and world.

The terrible possibility is that monotheism abstracted from the biblical revelation that engendered it can be conceived, and even believed in, in a way that complements and even reinforces such alienated spirituality. This is true of the traditional philosophical formulation of monotheism as one Substance which—or one Subject who—is the origin and measure of the many in the cosmos and as such is one, necessary, infinite, unconditional, immortal, and impassible. All these supposedly divine characteristics are derived by negating the characteristics of the finite, conditional, mortal, and passible (suffering) world. These cognitive negations are correlative with the spiritual alienation from the world that begets them. This theological approach to God is rightly called the "via negativa," for it is grounded in the negativity of spiritual alienation from one's world.

It makes little difference in the alienating character of this approach to God whether God is conceived as Substance or Subject. The conception of God as substance endured in Western history, especially under the influence of Aristotelian philosophy as long as the Greek sense of the cosmos as a house of being for the human soul continued. When our modern subjectivistic, empirical, pragmatic, technical approach to our world displaced it, the same conception of God now had to be elaborated as Subject to meet the Nietzschian kind of "atheism" that threatened to rise out of this loss of a cosmic sense of being: "Do we not feel the breath of empty space? Do we not continually encounter night and still more night? Do we not have to light our lanterns before noon? . . . God is dead! God remains dead! And we have killed him."[8]

For Christians, of course, even modern Christians, God was not dead. But their theology had to be reconceived. God could no longer be the absolute Substance grounding the cosmic house of being, so God was reconceived as the absolute Subject, similarly infinite, unconditioned, immortal, and impassible, as the ground of their subjectivity. Theology returned via Augustine to Plato and Neoplatonism and then moved forward with Kant, Schleiermacher, Lotze, and Kierkegaard to idealism, personal idealism, and existentialism. God is now the archetype of the soul—but, alas, of an alienated soul.

In this theological situation, the spiritual relation to the Holy Spirit could not be sensed or conceived as mediated through the whole of one's world, but only through one's experience of the self. Rudolf Bultmann perhaps put this more extravagantly than most: "For if the realization of our existence is involved in faith and if our existence is grounded in God and non-existent outside God, then to apprehend our existence means to apprehend God."[9] But the position of Karl Barth is little different at the point of his dependence upon the concept of the self to speak of God. More convinced than even Bultmann that God may not be known by any mediation of our sinful, alienated world, Barth conceives God as "wholly other" from it, so that God's revelation becomes strictly a "*self*-revelation" straight down from above. The essence of such self-revelation for Barth is God as "Lord":

> We may unhesitatingly equate the lordship of God, to which we found the whole of the biblical concept to be related, with what the vocabulary of the early church calls the essence of God, the *deitas* or *divinitas,* the divine *ousia, essentia, natura,* or *substantia.* . . The essence of God is the Godhead of God.[10]

The theological difference between Bultmann and Barth is in their understanding of the depth of spiritual alienation. Bultmann understands us to be alienated from our technocratic world, so our selfhood must be grounded directly through ourselves in God; Barth goes further and understands our selfhood itself to be alienated from God, so God's self-revelation must come to us from entirely beyond, not only our world but also ourselves. In both cases the self to whom revelation comes is the self spiritually alienated from its world; and thus the Self revealed in the Barthian God's self-revelation is, in my judgment, not the servant Self revealed in Jesus, or the Holy Spirit whose essence is love according to the New Testament, but far too much the alienated self of a "Lord"—a self-sufficient Lord whose infinite freedom is grounded in his eternal self-integration: "He could have remained satisfied with Himself and with the impassible glory and blessedness of His own inner life. But He did not do so. He elected man as a covenant-partner."[11]

Even a theologian like Paul Tillich, whose understanding of spirit and spiritual alienation has been followed closely in my own thought, remains too close to Barth's understanding of God's lordship at the central point of God's action. God is impassible even for Tillich, in the sense that God cannot be acted upon: "It should be regarded as the Protestant principle that, in relation to God, God alone can act, and that no human claim, especially no religious claim, no intellectual or moral or devotional 'work' can reunite us with him."[12]

These criticisms of great theologians, of course, should not be understood too comprehensively, as though there were nothing to learn from their doctrines of God and the Trinity; they are only directed at the one—but crucial—point of their understanding of God's unitary, active, impassible selfhood. This point is crucial to a dialectical theology of peace because so much depends here on understanding God's suffering. To conceive God as an all-active, self-sufficient, impassible "Lord" is to deny God any internal relation to our world's history in which God suffers the suffering of our world. It is Jürgen Moltmann again, in my judgment, who best understands what is at stake theologically in this issue:

> If a person experiences in faith how God has experienced— and still experiences—him, for that person God is not the abstract origin of the world, or the unknown source of his absolute feeling of dependency; he is *the living* God. He learns to know himself in the mirror of God's love, suffering, and joy. . . . He then perceives that the history of the world is the history of God's suffering. At the moments of God's profoundest revelation there is always suffering: the cry of the captives in Egypt; Jesus' death cry on the cross; the sighing of the whole enslaved creation for liberty. If a person once feels the infinite passion of God's love which finds expression here, then he understands the mystery of the triune God. God suffers with us—God suffers from us—God suffers for us: it is this experience of God that reveals the triune God.[13]

To enter into renewed relation with God whose very being is constituted relationally as Father, Son, and Holy Spirit is to find a new ultimate basis for one's peaceful relation to the world. No matter how demonic the distortions of that world, no matter how real the alienation from it, one finds here no basis for capitulating to, withdrawing from, or lording over the world. When the Son who accepted the suffering caused by demonic forces of human alienation is believed to be eternally in relation to the Father, and when the Holy Spirit who relates us to God, to the other faithful, and reconcilingly to our whole world is believed to be the eternal Spirit that relates the Father and the Son, then we have an ultimate basis for dialectical peace. Dialectical peace, here as before, means a reconciled relationship with God that brings integral personal peace, creates reconciled communities, and energizes a renewed nonviolent struggle to transform the demonic structures that block social peace and even distort our human efforts to achieve it.

A monotheistic belief in God can seek and has sought to bring universal peace to the world. Christendom, both in the Holy Roman Empire and Byzantium, sought to be a universal religion of peace, grounded in an absolute monotheism and expressed through a sovereign emperor more akin to a Davidic royal messiah than to Jesus Christ. Christendom's understanding of peace was more direct than dialectical, reflecting its belief in the sovereign monarchy of God more than God's trinitarian social relationality, which was revealed in Christ and the Holy Spirit as taking the suffering struggle of the world into itself and transforming it through divine gracious power into forgiveness and new possibility.

> As long as the unity of the triune God is understood monadically or subjectivistically, and not in trinitarian terms, the whole cohesion of a religious legitimation of political sovereignty continues to exist. It is only when the doctrine of the Trinity vanquishes the monotheistic notion of the great universal monarch in heaven, and his divine patriarchs in the world, that earthly rulers, dictators and tyrants cease to find any justifying religious archetypes any more.[14]

Human Participation in the Trinitarian Spirit of Peace

The trinitarian understanding of the Holy Spirit we are developing here uses analogies of human sociality, more prevalent in Eastern Orthodox theologies, to complement the analogies drawn from human individuality, more characteristic of Western theology since Augustine. Augustine's concept of the triune God who is at the same time Lover, Beloved, and Love is biblically grounded in the revelation of God's love in Jesus Christ, but it seeks to interpret God's Being with psychological analogies of our human capacity to differentiate, objectify, and affirm ourselves in the I-me relation.[15] In this case, the Holy Spirit is understood as the Love that the "self-sufficient" God has in and for God's interiorly, or immanently, differentiated Self. In contrast, the Cappadocian theologians understood God's Being to be constituted by the community of three Persons, each with their own hypostasis, so that their unity is constituted socially.[16]

The accusation of "tritheism," leveled at this concept by monotheists, misses the mark, because this theology never thought of the three Persons of the Trinity as three individuals who only subsequently related to each other. The three divine Persons were understood to be socially constituted eternally by their relations to each other. The traditional technical term expressing this concept of the Trinity's social being was *perichoresis* in Greek and *circumincessio* in Latin. This concept seeks to express an understanding of the divine Persons as living in an eternal process of an exchange of energies or, alternately expressed, as a process of "mutual immanence in the divine nature."[17] The analogy from the human level is our experience of genuine empathy, raised in the Cappadocian concept of the Trinity to an eternal process of perfect empathy.

This concept of the social relationality and perichoretic unity of the Trinity is clearly analogous to the notion of the human spirit I developed earlier as an integrating center of dynamic relationships, in which the hypostasis of a person is understood to be the spiritual center of natural and social relations. As human beings, however, we actualize such unity only spasmodically and fragmentarily. As finite spiritual centers our integration is momentary and limited. Our spiritual integration is a spatiotemporal event that becomes and perishes and in varying degrees is distorted by our personal alienations and the influences upon us of demonic structures of nationalism, racism, sexism, and class conflict. For such spirits as we are to have faith in Jesus Christ and receive the Holy Spirit through him is to be drawn into the trinitarian life of God. It is to participate in the love of the Trinity. It is to have our finite centers ecstatically opened to the relational life of God, so that our alienations and demonic distortions may be healed and overcome. Our limited relationality and ideologically distorted sociality is saved from the fears and hostilities it otherwise engenders. Insofar, then, as we spiritually integrate ourselves with the Holy Spirit, who is perichoretically the Spirit of the universal Creator and suffering Redeemer, we find ourselves at personal peace with the whole creation and sharing the social passion of the Redeemer to bring the whole creation to universal peace.

I intend to develop the universality of peace grounded in the community of the Trinity more completely and systematically in the next chapter, where I also must develop the concept of the unity of Christ Jesus as a fully human, particular person united with the eternal Son, understood as the universal Logos of creation. It now remains to show more concretely what it is to participate in the Holy Spirit of peace.

The recent reflections of M. L. Brownsberger, who is both a theologically trained, ordained Presbyterian minister and the vice-president for finance of a pharmaceutical manufacturing company in Chicago, provide an excellent opportunity for more concrete illustration. I wish to respond because in some ways I share Mr. Brownsberger's lament over the "trained incapacity" of most pastors to relate their theology to the work experience of those like him whose lives are set in the American political economy. He describes the "public life" Americans share as characterized by "four realities":

> First, our willingness and ability to live with contradictions; second, the reality of institutionalized disharmony; third, the belief that lived truth is a function of debate; and fourth, the belief that consensus is only occasional, serial and episodic, and is the basis for subsequent disagreement.[18]

The consequence of living in this North American capitalist context is "disharmony," which Mr. Brownsberger experiences as "the energy of the system, the model and perhaps the procedural principle not only of our polity but also of our economics and our culture, including our churches." We have institutionalized a social system where "ambition must be made to counter ambition" (James Madison) and "clashing with each other almost without cease is the expected daily routine" (Robert Goldwin).[19]

From the christological and trinitarian perspective I have been developing, Mr. Brownsberger graphically describes the experience of alienated, individualistic spirits, estranged from each other and God's Holy Spirit in a competitive society. However, as a Christian acculturated in American civil religion, he experiences and interprets it more positively as incorporating the values of pluralism and diversity that American Christians have been taught to affirm. Thus he turns to the biblical story of the tower of Babel and the Christian faith in the Holy Spirit to understand what he calls

"God's Babel effort to make and keep human life human" in this competitive context. He interprets the Babel story in Genesis 11, where God confounds human language so that people may no longer understand each other, as more blessing than punishment. It is God's way of keeping us from successful idolatry; God renders the idolatry of pretentious tower-building "disharmonious and plural," saving us from our cruel utopianisms by maintaining diversity. And Luke's account of the gift of the Holy Spirit in Acts 2 is seen as reinforcing this pluralistic diversity:

> In plurality there is a spirit that energizes the various elements. The Pentecostal spirit is released in the tongues of a plural people, who occasionally build new towers and then flatten them with new forms of creativity. The spirit is loose in a land in which the people clash "almost without cease."[20]

Mr. Brownsberger hopes that this theological interpretation will foster "moral integration" and personal responsibility. One need not and should not denigrate the values of individual personality, diversity, and pluralism that he seeks to affirm in order to reject his strange interpretation of the gift of the Holy Spirit. It is clear on the face of Luke's account in Acts 2 that the gift of the Holy Spirit reverses the loss of communication and community that humanity suffered in the Babel story. Now "the mighty works of God" in Jesus Christ are communicated by Galileans "as the Spirit gave them utterance," so that people of every tongue in the then known world heard them speaking in their "own native languages." Acts 2 is manifestly not a continuation but a reversal of Genesis 11. The Holy Spirit enables a universal empathy and communication, so that one need not any longer safeguard the pluralistic values of finite spirits by ceaseless competition and conflict. One may now know a "moral integration," to use Mr. Brownsberger's excellent term, that energizes and enables one to seek a social peace on a universal scale without idolatry. To know the true trinitarian God of universal love is to be delivered from our demonic national, racial, sexual, class, and personal competitive idolatries. To receive the Holy Spirit is to participate in the spirit of peace.

Jürgen Moltmann understands the values of finite personality that Mr. Brownsberger and I seek to affirm and protect as grounded in the doctrine of the Trinity:

> In the Western church's doctrine of the Trinity the concept of Person was developed with particular emphasis. This had a strongly formative effect on Western anthropology. If today we understand person as the unmistakable and untransferable individual existence, we owe this to the Christian doctrine of the Trinity.[21]

Thus pluralistic diversity grounded in individual integrity is to be affirmed and protected where need be. But Moltmann also sees the strange distortion of Brownsberger's interpretation as grounded in an inadequate understanding of the Trinity widespread in our churches:

> But why was the concept of the *perichoresis*—the unity and fellowship of the Persons—not developed with equal emphasis? The disappearance of the social doctrine of the Trinity has made room for the development of individualism, and especially "possessive individualism," in the Western world: everyone is supposed to fulfill himself, but who fulfills the community? It is a typically Western bias to suppose that social relationships and society are less "primal" than the person.[22]

I am convinced with Moltmann that when the Christian doctrine of the Trinity and the Holy Spirit are understood as I have tried to articulate them, "personalism and socialism cease to be antitheses and are seen to be derived from a common foundation."[23] All of us are called to help develop a social personalism, or personal socialism, and thus create peace in our alienated, competitive, and conflicted world.

5

The Unity of Christ, Community of Trinity, and Universality of Peace

The complex theme of this chapter indicates that we now have before us, as developed in the previous chapters, the conceptual elements whose coherent interpretation may enable the more comprehensive understanding of peace that our world so desperately needs. The spirit of the fully human Jewish Jesus, crucified in and by the demonic conflicts of our peaceless world and resurrected in the trinitarian being of the eternal, creative, and reconciling God, may and must be interpreted as the meaning of, and means toward, universal peace.

The operative concepts here are manifestly unity, community, and universality, which interpret the Christian's experience of the peace of Christ as objectively grounded in the trinitarian being of God. To understand the *unity* of Christ overcomes and sets aside all forms of ontological dualism—whether the Manichean of good and evil, the Gnostic of spirit and matter, the Thomistic of natural and supernatural, the Augustinian/Lutheran of the kingdoms of earth and heaven, the Kantian/liberal of phenomenal and noumenal reality, or the apocalyptic dispensationalist of two or more ages—when they are used or abused to suggest that the peace of Christ is reserved for some other time or place than the creative and responsible moment in which Christians now live.

This, of course, cannot mean that every theological insight expressed through these dualisms is to be repudiated. If nothing else, their very long and continuing history in the church's life is sufficient evidence that these various dualistic formulations interpret important dimensions of the Christian experience of reality. Ethical differentiation of good and evil is obviously crucial to the Christian understanding of peace. Ontological differentiation of human spirits and the divine Spirit from other dimensions of the creation is essential to actualizing Christian existence and the praxis of peace. Historical differentiation on the basis of Jesus Christ's real incarnation in humanity's social process is necessary to clearly interpret the Christian meaning of, and impact on, humanity's peace.

Thus a relative dualism interpreting a dialectical understanding of peace is the most coherent concept for a christologically based interpretation of peace. All absolute dualisms, however, that divide humanity from Deity by some "wholly other" (Barth), or time from eternity by some "infinite qualitative distinction" (Kierkegaard), or the secular from the sacred, in the pietism or the civil religion of so many in our day, must be resisted and corrected. The way toward such correction, in my judgment, runs from the Chalcedonian understanding of Christ's unity through contemporary reformulations of the Logos Christology that has always constituted its base. The theological goal is so adequate an understanding of the gift and demand of Christ's peace in our historical existence that we may joyously and responsibly practice it.

This christological unity, however, is realized, celebrated, and practiced in Christian community. It does not give rise to or eventuate in some mystical unity beyond the pluralisms of human finitude. The highest form of Christian unity is precisely community because the being of the creative God with whom we are being reconciled is communal. Our God is trinitarian. There is no way to realize at-one-ment with the trinitarian God revealed in Jesus Christ other than through at-with-ment with the neighbor. We cannot love the trinitarian God with all that we are without loving the neighbors God has given. To fail to forgive them is to forfeit God's forgiveness of us. To be in Christ is to be with them. To receive the Holy Spirit is to unite our spirit with their spirits in community.

Yet none of our communities even approximates the universal. To heal the excess of human egoism in limited community is to open ourselves to the far greater danger of the alter-egoism of families, races, classes, nation-states, and even churches. To become more moral persons in finite communities may ironically and tragically only contribute to their competing immoralities. The oft-repeated story of humanity, from Confucian bureaucrats to Christian chancellors and almost every good parent, is that we will do in good conscience for our community what we would consider unconscionable if done only for ourselves.

We shall adequately understand and practice the peace of Christ only when the unity that Christ gives with the trinitarian God leads us toward universal community. Only when we profoundly understand that there is one Creator at work through one Logos in the whole creation to bring it to communion through one Spirit will we be drawn into our finite communities without succumbing to the sinful dynamics of their alter-egoisms. Then we may elaborate our human ideas without absolutist ideologies, our national cultures without idolatrous civil cults, our human laws without destructive legalisms, our human economies without forgetfulness of nature's ecology, and our religious communities without divisively absolute claims. To realize the unity of Christ and our unity with Christ in the community of the Trinity is the way toward universal peace.

The Unity of Christ as the Logos of Creation

The concern for peace in a peaceless world faces Christians with a crisis of truth. Is the peace that Christ gives in some sense an opium for human spirits—a soporific to dull the cruel edges of reality—or is it the ultimate truth for the fulfillment of all life? Perhaps not all of us reflect on this crisis in a context so dramatic as Dostoevski when he returned from his prison of forced labor in Siberia, but we all have known those aspects of our world that make it a "house of the dead," so we can identify with what he beautifully expressed to Baronesa von Wizine:

> At times God sends me moments of peace; on these occasions, I love and feel that I am loved; it was in one such moment that I composed for myself a credo in which all is clear and sacred. This credo is very simple. This is it: I believe that there is nothing on earth more beautiful, more profound, more appealing, more virile, or more perfect than Christ; and I say to myself with jealous love, that greater than he does

not and cannot exist. More than this: should anyone prove
to me that Christ is beyond the range of truth, and that all
this is not to be found in him, I would prefer to retain Christ
than to retain the truth.[1]

Is the peace of Christ the truth? Can the credos in which we
express it make "*all* clear and sacred," or must we sacrifice the
truth "to retain Christ"? Though few can even attempt to unite
authentic faith with articulated worldview in a way that fully
answers this question, the commitment of Christian theology from
its beginnings in the New Testament kerygma is clear: Jesus the
Christ is the ultimate truth of all reality as the Logos of creation,
and he will lead it to its fulfillment in peace.

We have developed in chapter 2 the exegetical basis for identify-
ing Jesus in the kerygma of the Gospels as the expected eschatological prophet interpreted as the Solomonic Son of David, who both
announced and manifested in his ministry the eschatological reign
of God. This charismatic hermeneusis, analogous to the Jewish
hermeneutic that used Moses, Elijah, and Enoch as literary figures
to interpret their contemporary eschatological hopes, was adopted
by first-century Christians to interpret Jesus' life, death, and resurrection as the source of their faith movement. To interpret Jesus
as the Solomonic Son of David was to reject the royal messianism
that inspired the Zealot movement of his and their day in favor of
understanding Jesus through the symbols of their Wisdom tradition.

Israel's Wisdom tradition had related Deutero-Isaiah's servant
of God to the suffering expression of God's wisdom in the world
(Wisd. of Sol. 2:3). "Ungodly men" (1:16) "reasoned unsoundly"
(2:1), it was said, in a way that prefigures the New Testament's
depiction of Jesus' life experience as God's wise and suffering
servant:

He calls the last end of the righteous happy,
  and boasts that God is his father.
Let us see if his words are true,
  and let us test what will happen at the end of his life;
for if the righteous man is God's son, he will help him,
  and will deliver him from the hand of his adversaries.
Let us test him with insult and torture,

> that we may find out how gentle he is,
> and make trial of his forbearance.
> Let us condemn him to a shameful death,
> for, according to what he says, he will be protected.
>
> Wisdom of Solomon 2:16–20

Thus it was not a large step for the Gospel writers to interpret Jesus as the Wisdom of God who revealed in his life, death, and resurrection "the secret purposes of God" (Wisd. of Sol. 2:22), though hidden from those whose "wickedness blinded them" (2:21). Edward Schillebeeckx has summarized this transition with remarkable clarity:

> The awareness grew . . . that in Jesus God's final revelation of salvation had taken place and that the revelation of salvation surpassed the wisdom in the Torah. However, the Torah and the wisdom of God which speaks of it had already been regarded as pre-existent. Jesus' superiority to the revelation of salvation in the Law thus almost automatically implied the notion of pre-existence, in the sense of existing before all creation, and finally also in the sense of being mediator at creation—designations which had earlier been applied to the revelation of wisdom in the Law. By taking over these predicates, Christians had demonstrated that for them *Jesus* was the eschatological, i.e., the full and final, revelation of God's salvation. This is also the fundamental purpose of the whole of the Gospel of John. Paul had already said the same thing: "Through him you are in Christ Jesus, who has become *our whole wisdom from God, our righteousness, sanctification and redemption*" (1 Cor. 1:30). For John, Jesus himself is the gospel, the message, "the word."[2]

John's concept of the divine Logos in his Gospel's prologue must be understood in this context of Israel's Wisdom tradition, rather than any hypothetical context of Gnostic redeemer myths. The Johannine Logos is not a Gnostic mediator between God and the world but is spoken of as both simply God and with God.[3] As such, he is both the mediator of creation and its redeemer:

> In the beginning was the Word, and the Word was with God, and the Word was God. He was in the beginning with God; all things were made through him, and without him was not anything made that was made. . . . And the Word became

> flesh and dwelt among us, full of grace and truth. . . . And
> from his fulness have we all received, grace upon grace.
>
> John 1:1–3, 14, 16

The later Chalcedonian and trinitarian christological formulations are already implicit here: The Christ who became flesh is
God, with the suggestion ("with God") of differentiation in God's
being. As such, Christ is Creator—the Wisdom or Logos which
orders creation to its divine end—and Christ is Redeemer, who
graciously restores and renews creation when it has fallen away
from God's creative purpose.

The New Testament concept of Christ as the Logos of creation
is not as exclusive to the Johannine witness as is sometimes
thought. It is already in the earlier letters of Paul: "There is one
Lord, Jesus Christ, through whom are all things and through
whom we exist" (1 Cor. 8:6). The later Pauline or Deutero-Pauline
letter to the Colossians develops this concept more extensively:

> He is the image of the invisible God, the first-born of all
> creation; for in him all things were created, in heaven and on
> earth, visible and invisible, whether thrones or dominions or
> principalities or authorities—all things were created through
> him and for him. He is before all things, and in him all things
> hold together.
>
> Colossians 1:15–17

And it is precisely because Christ is the Logos of creation that the
author of Colossians can understand the resurrected Christ as
reconciling all things, thus creating universal peace: "For in him
all the fulness of God was pleased to dwell, and through him to
reconcile to himself all things, whether on earth or in heaven,
making peace by the blood of his cross" (1:19–20).

The book of Hebrews also reflects this universal Logos Christology: "But in these last days God has spoken to us by a Son,
whom he appointed the heir of all things, through whom also he
created the world. He reflects the glory of God and bears the very
stamp of his nature, upholding the universe by his word of power"
(Heb. 1:2–3). It also is found in Q, the sayings source used by the
authors of Matthew and Luke, especially in the reaction to those
who show that they do not know the wisdom of God by their
rejection of Jesus.[4]

It is in the letter to the churches of Asia Minor, known as Ephesians, that we find the fullest development of this Logos theme related to our focus on peace. Ephesians' key concept is *eirene,* or peace. The gospel that Christ preached was peace: "He came and preached peace to you who were far off and peace to those who were near" (2:17). By breaking down the dividing wall of hostility between Greek and Jew in Asia Minor, Christ "is our peace" (2:14). If we allow our spirits to be armored with truth, righteousness, and faith, this "gospel of peace" will enable us to stand and withstand the hard struggle against the peaceless powers of darkness in this world (6:10–17).

This focus on peace in Ephesians is the concrete implication for Christians of Christ as the Logos of creation:

> For he [the God and Father of our Lord Jesus Christ] has made known to us in all wisdom and insight the mystery of his will, according to his purpose which he set forth in Christ as a plan for the fulness of time, to unite all things in him, things in heaven and things on earth.
>
> Ephesians 1:9–10

The theology suggested and developed in Ephesians is so foundational to a Christology of peace that I fully agree with Professor Schillebeeckx's judgment: "If any book lays the foundation for a political theology in the New Testament, it is Ephesians," though he qualifies it by adding that "the author himself does not see through its historical consequences or implications."[5] Be that as it may, the religious basis for the church's peace witness is entirely clear in Ephesians: the church must express the new possibility of reconciliation and peace for all humanity through common access to the one God who has entered our history to forgive sin and renew life.

The courageous hope expressed in Ephesians, which called the minuscule first-century Christian communities of Asia Minor to become the expressions of God's universal peace within and against the Roman Empire, remains a canonical challenge to the cautious if not cowardly political timidity of twentieth-century churches in a thermonuclear age characterized by cold war. Many act as though they perhaps had never heard that God's reconciling purpose revealed in Christ is to unite all things in him in peace; or, if they have heard, they have not understood; or, if they have understood, they do not intend to obey.

This indictment, however, is too bold and unqualified. One of the qualifications surely is theological, in that one or another of the theological dualisms named at the beginning of this chapter qualifies much contemporary understanding of the biblical message I have been tracing through Paul, Q, John, and the Deutero-Pauline epistles. So the peace of Christ is interpreted as spiritual in contrast to political, to be fully known only "above" in heaven or "at the end" in the future eschaton, though it may meanwhile be pietistically cherished in our "hearts" if it does not lead us to disturb the "peace through strength" political strategies promulgated on the basis of fear and hatred of our enemies by our civil religion.

Though the issue resolved at Chalcedon between Alexandrian and Antiochian theologians was quite different, in that it dealt metaphysically with the duality of Christ's natures being united in the unity of his person, the soteriological concern is clearly analogous. Criteria were established so that whatever is attributed to Jesus' complete humanity, on the one hand, or to his true deity, on the other, must be simultaneously affirmed without dividing or compromising his fundamental unity:

> [We declare that] he is not parted or separated into two persons, but one and the same Son and only begotten God the Word, Lord Jesus Christ; even as the prophets from earliest times spoke of him and our Lord Jesus Christ himself taught us, and the creed of the Fathers has handed down to us.[6]

This formula of unity fulfilled the fundamental soteriological principle first articulated in the pre-Chalcedonian theological struggle by Gregory of Nazianzus: "That which God did not assume, he also did not redeem. If the Logos did not assume the human spirit, it was not redeemed."[7] The grave theological danger averted at Chalcedon was that the power and purpose of God's Logos of creation would be sundered in the church's theology from the concrete creativity, suffering, and struggle of humanity that God had fully "assumed" in Jesus the Christ. When the church follows the criteria of Chalcedon to allow no dualism to sunder what God has united in Christ, then every religious, saving, integrating, reconciling impulse Christians receive through Jesus will be fully mediated into the sociopolitical process whereby they seek peace. Whatever proper critical role may yet be exercised by the "eschatological reservation" based on God's transcendence, it may no longer be used to deny or divert the church's concrete witness to the "peace of Christ" as canonically grounded in the Logos Christology of the New Testament.

Contemporary Christians and churches, however, do not find every issue resolved by scripture and tradition. Though one may finally agree that the peace achieved through the Logos of creation is a fundamental motif of the New Testament, and that the Chalcedonian definition protects its theological relevance for our human struggles for peace, some still may find the notion of the Logos unintelligible in contemporary terms and the dogmatic authority of Chalcedon superseded by contemporary reason and experience. John Cobb comments in this regard:

> Protestant scholarship has done little toward a transformation of the positive meaning of Chalcedon. When Chalcedon is accepted, the acceptance is in terms of a supernatural and sacred Jesus and an exclusivist faith. When Chalcedon is rejected, the interpretation of its meaning is the same. The radical historical scholarship that has freed the meaning of the New Testament from its alien world view, from its supernaturalism and exclusivism, and has thus made it accessible to contemporary consciousness, has largely passed Chalcedon by.[8]

Current-day conceptual difficulties in interpreting the Logos Christology that is the basis for Chalcedon's affirmation of "God the Word" are articulated by Wolfhart Pannenberg:

> If one wished to reproduce an analogy to the patristic Logos Christology, namely, in connection with the contemporary thought of natural science, one would have to begin by understanding the laws of nature, contrary to the self-understanding of natural science, as prototypes existing beyond and not fully expressed in the natural processes. The whole experimental methodology of our modern understanding of nature resists such an interpretation.[9]

Pannenberg has in mind the Platonic and Stoic Logos concepts of hellenistic cosmology, where the Logos was understood as the eternal world-reason that held the cosmos together by setting matter in motion and giving it form. Pannenberg complains that this philosophical concept of God's Logos retained too much influence, not only in patristic theology but down to today. It should have been more fully reformulated than it has been by the church's faith in the revelation of the Logos in Jesus. Pannenberg argues:

> The one God is revealed in the person and history of Jesus differently than he had been conceived by philosophy. He is revealed, not as the unchangeable ultimate ground of the phenomenal order, but as the free origin of the contingent events of the world, whose interrelations are also contingent and constitute no eternal order but a history moving forward from event to event.[10]

John Cobb has attempted the most sustained reformulation of the Logos concept for contemporary Christology. He, like Pannenberg, is concerned that the "substantialist categories" used by the church fathers caused the church to retain "ideas of the Logos uncongenial to what is apparent in Jesus"—that is, to try to think of him as "the unchanging wisdom and will of God."[11] The motive for continuing the reconception of the Logos in the direction begun at Chalcedon, so that it is no longer thought of as an unchangeable ultimate ground for unchanging essences or substances, is seen both as bringing theology closer to God's revelation in Jesus and as making it more coherent with the contemporary scientific understanding of nature. The fact that Cobb's metaphysical mentor, the mathematician and philosopher of science Alfred North Whitehead, thought the Chalcedonian theologians to "have the distinction of being the only thinkers who in a fundamental metaphysical doctrine have improved upon Plato,"[12] provides the bridge between these two motives. The trinitarian understanding of "mutual immanence in the divine nature," the Chalcedonian understanding of the "direct immanence of God in the one person of Christ," and the correlative understanding of the Holy Spirit as the "direct immanence of God in the world generally" were all seen by Whitehead as pointing the way for metaphysics to develop in order to "give a rational account of the role of the persuasive agency of God."[13]

It is exactly God's persuasive agency in the world as the Logos of creation that we are concerned to understand as the basis for the church's peace witness and praxis. Therefore, our conception of the Logos must be understood in the light of Jesus' historical birth, growth, teaching, suffering, death, and resurrection. It no longer may be conceived as an eternal, unchanging order but must be rethought in some such dynamic terms as "the not-yet-realized [which is] transforming the givenness of the past from a burden into a potentiality for new creation." Such a theological concept provides a more adequate basis for the church's commitment to what Cobb designates as the "unrealized potentiality for transforming the world without destroying it."[14] His understanding of the Logos as "creative transformation" provides a contemporary way to understand the unity of Christ and our unity in Christ as the ground for both personal and sociopolitical peace.

John Cobb's ontological interpretation of the Logos is congruent with Pannenberg's view of "history moving forward from event to event" in a way that does not contradict the experimental methodologies of contemporary natural science, while rejecting earlier materialistic and mechanistic scientific models. Thus he rejects an earlier scientific worldview that reductively interpreted all purposive phenomena as caused by antecedent conditions:

> Each momentary experience can be seen as the meeting place of past actuality experienced as the demand for some measure of conformation and certain unrealized possibilities experienced as worthy of actualization. The aim at becoming—and at becoming in such a way as to achieve some optimum of satisfaction, immediately and also for the sake of a wider future—is a factor in human experience that should not be reduced to the conformal pressures of the past. It is the principle of novelty, spontaneity, growth and self-transcendence. It is that element in experience by which a continuing restlessness is introduced into the human race, a refusal of mere acquiescence in the given.[15]

This phenomenological validation that some or all events may creatively transform the inherited past by actualizing not-yet-realized possibilities is interpreted by Cobb, following Whitehead, as actualizing the immanent "initial aim" of the transcendent Logos.[16] Whitehead's analysis of the "immediacy of a concrescent fact" puts it this way:

> The initial stage of its aim is an endowment which the subject inherits from the inevitable ordering of things, conceptually realized in the nature of God. . . . In this sense, God is the principle of concretion; namely he is that actual entity from which each temporal concrescence receives that initial aim from which its self-causation starts. . . . Thus the transition of the creativity from an actual world to the correlate novel concrescence is conditioned by the relevance of God's all-embracing conceptual valuations to the particular possibilities of transmission from the actual world, and by its relevance to the various possibilities of initial subjective form available for the initial feelings.[17]

John Cobb relates this metaphysical insight to the Logos tradition of Christian theology, interpreting the immanence of the transcendent Logos as a "special case of causal efficacy in general."[18] This becomes intelligible as we replace metaphysical and common-sense notions of substance with a metaphysics of dynamic events that may be understood as integrating many internal relations into a new synthesis in each new occasion. The Logos may then be understood as that dimension of God's being which is "the order of unrealized potentiality making possible by its immanence the realization of novel order."[19] This potentiality interacts with the statistically dominant patterns and tendencies of myriad past events to lure each event toward its optimum possible form at that point in the spatiotemporal process. At the level of human experience, we sense this interaction with the past as the struggle with habit, anxiety, and defensiveness, grounded in inertia and entropy. Christ then may be succinctly understood as "creative transformation as the incarnation of the Logos."[20]

The existential correlate of this ontological insight is an openness to the future that delivers us from bondage to the past. We learn to trust the life-transforming lure that calls us from whatever security we have personally achieved or have been socially given, in the confidence that our future in common with the transformed future of all others will be richer and more satisfying. The conscious and unconscious memory of the chain of experiences of our personal and social past need not be completely constitutive of our present selfhood; we may transcend the socialization of our ethnic and national cultures. Thus we may be, and in some ways remain, Jew or Greek, Russian or American, while being more fully constituted by our response to the lure of creative transformation that is the immanent Logos. John Cobb interprets the structure of Jesus' historical existence as the perfect instance of this existential possibility:

> The "I" in each moment is constituted as much in the subjective reception of the lure to self-actualization that is the call and the presence of the Logos as it is in continuity with the personal past. This structure of existence would be the incarnation of the Logos in the fullest meaningful sense.[21]

Jesus is the Christ because his "I" was co-constituted by the incarnate Logos.

John Cobb's understanding of the Logos, revealed through its incarnation in Jesus as a perfect instance of that creative transformation universally incarnated in a dynamic world process of spatiotemporal events, provides, in my judgment, the contemporary interpretation of the unity of Christ and the possibility of our unity in Christ that the church needs in order intelligibly to affirm the Logos of creation as the ground for personal and sociopolitical peace. But there is a momentous omission in Cobb's discussion that disguises and limits its helpfulness for articulating this concern for peace. When he discusses the dominant patterns and tendencies of past events and their existential correlates of habit, defensiveness, and anxiety, he thinks only in terms of entropy and inertia while virtually ignoring the fatal reality of conflict and violence. Thus his Christology focuses on Jesus' teaching and person while failing to deal adequately with his crucifixion. This is even astonishingly the case when he deals with the Pauline understanding of Christ's work, which he reduces to a discussion of Paul's "Christ-mysticism" as a historical field of force. As illuminating as this discussion is in its own right, it simply bypasses the Pauline focus on understanding Jesus as Christ crucified.

Thus, Cobb provides us little help in articulating the peculiarly dialectical understanding of peace that must come to terms with the conflict, violence, and death that so tragically constitute a major dimension of "the patterns and tendencies of past events" in our yet peaceless world.[22] Though he rejects any analogy between a Davidic kind of kingly power and God's power, he stays too close to its correlated theological position that understands the whole world process as an expression of God's providential power. The inadequacy of Cobb's position in failing to recognize the demonic that has emerged in history is clear when he writes:

> The order in the past world derives from the ordering power of the Logos. . . . Every event inherits dominant patterns from the past, but insofar as those patterns are not eternal, all arose originally in the response of many events to the possibilities of order derived from the Logos.[23]

It is necessary to go beyond this form of simple panentheism to the dialectical panentheism of Jürgen Moltmann, as interpreted in chapter 3. The perfect instance of creative transformation in the Logos' incarnation in Jesus, after all, was actualized in our conflicted world only through Jesus' death and resurrection. Thus God must be seen as suffering the violent conflict caused by demonic structures emergent through fallen finite freedom in world history, which may live from the order derived from the Logos, as Cobb contends, but only while deeply distorting and destroying that order in a way that he does not fully recognize.

Moltmann is so impressed with the radically negative meaning of the crucifixion that he understands God the Father as "abandoning" Jesus on the cross.

> Thus in the total, inextricable abandonment of Jesus by his God and Father, Paul sees the delivering up of the Son by the Father for godless and godforsaken man. Because God "does not spare" his Son, all the godless are spared. Though they are godless, they are not godforsaken, precisely because God has abandoned his own Son and has delivered him up for them. . . . It may therefore be said that the Father delivers up his Son on the cross in order to be the Father of those who are delivered up.[24]

Though it must be recognized that Moltmann is only interpreting Pauline texts in Romans 8:31, 2 Corinthians 5:21, and Galatians 3:13, the theological formulation that God "abandoned" Jesus to the cross, unless meant as a metaphor not to be taken seriously, has dualistic implications that strike me as too extreme. It suggests that the demonic dimensions of our world are so powerful as to force division in God's very being.

This is clearly not Moltmann's intention. He wants to interpret the cross in trinitarian terms as an event in the loving relation between the Son and the Father:

> The Son suffers in his love being forsaken by the Father as he dies. The Father suffers in his love the grief of the death of the Son. In that case, whatever proceeds from the event between the Father and the Son must be understood as the spirit of the surrender of the Father and the Son, or the spirit which creates love for forsaken men, as the spirit which brings the dead alive.[25]

The trinitarian form of Moltmann's understanding must be affirmed. The crucifixion of Jesus the Christ is an expression of the love between the Father and the Son, now become suffering love as the incarnate Logos is crucified in a violently demonic world. The negativity of our sinful world does enter into and affect the very being and becoming of God. But the historical phenomenon revealed in the New Testament witness is the loving obedience of Jesus as the incarnate Logos, who takes the *consequences* of our world's demonic divisions into himself and thus takes those consequences into God, but it is not necessary also to postulate that the very division caused by historical demonic structures is thereby also taken into God. The incarnate hypostasis of the Logos in Jesus may not be able to see the eschatological end at the moment of his agony, but he faithfully accepts the divine aim that takes him to his death. This is clearly the testimony of the Last Supper as Jesus faced Gethsemane and Golgotha.[26]

Cobb's understanding of the Logos as creative transformation may thus be assimilated to that of the crucified Christ in Moltmann.[27] One need not accept the implications of extreme dualism in some of Moltmann's formulations to move to his profound deepening of process theology's panentheism in his notion of dialectical panentheism. Moltmann's profound insight is deeply needed for the church's theology of peace. I know of no theologian who has stated it better:

"God *is* love," says 1 John 4:16. Thus in view of all that has been said, the doctrine of the Trinity can be understood as an interpretation of the ground, the event and the experience of that love in which the one who has been condemned to love finds new possibility for life. . . . It is not the interpretation of love as an ideal, a heavenly power or as a commandment, but of love as an event in a loveless, legalistic world: the event of an unconditioned and boundless love which comes to meet man, which takes hold of those who are unloved and forsaken, unrighteous or outside the law, and gives them a new identity, liberates them from the norms of social identification and from the guardians of social norms and idolatrous images. What Jesus commanded on the Sermon on the Mount as love of one's enemies has taken place on the cross through Jesus' dying and the grief of the Father in the power of the spirit, for the godless and the loveless. . . . The fact of this love can be contradicted. It can be crucified, but in crucifixion it finds its fulfillment and becomes love of the enemy. Thus its suffering proves to be stronger than hate. Its might is powerful in weakness and gives power over its enemies in grief because it gives life even to its enemies and opens up the future to change.[28]

This is the theological summation of the life, teaching, death, and resurrection of Jesus, the crucified and resurrected incarnate Logos of creation, as the ground for the Christian gospel of peace.

The Community of the Trinity and the Process of Peace

To have our spirit integrated through the lure of the Logos of creation understood through the crucified and resurrected Christ is to know the Holy Spirit as the Spirit of the universal Creator and suffering Redeemer. This is the Christian experience of coming to personal peace with the whole, though conflicted, creation, and of thereby sharing the social passion of the Redeemer to reconcile the whole conflicted creation in universal peace. I argued in chapter 4 that it is the social analogies, more characteristic of Eastern theology, that more adequately interpret these trinitarian terms as community, rather than the psychological analogies that Western theology more characteristically uses to interpret the Trinity as person. In other words, it is important for the theology of peace that the unity of God's being be understood as constituted socially rather than personally. We can realize God's peace as differentiated persons only in the actualization of community, because we are created in the image of the trinitarian God and are lured to panentheistic participation in the social process that is grounded in God's trinitarian being.

There is no doubt that the doctrine of the Trinity developed in the church's attempt to understand the relation of God to what was understood as incarnately actualized in Jesus. A Christology based on the sapiential Logos allowed the affirmation that what was incarnate in Jesus was divine. But it was divine precisely as Logos in distinction from God the Creator/Father and God the Holy Spirit. And it is in interpreting these distinctions that deep variations have emerged in the church's trinitarian theologies.

The significance of these disagreements for the theology of peace may again be illustrated by examining John Cobb's theology and particularly his judgment that "the doctrine of the Trinity tended to become a mystification rather than a clarification of Christian belief."[29] The conceptuality that Cobb finds clarifying is a modalism that understands the one God "as expressing himself through Logos, or Son, and Spirit."[30] What he finds "mystifying" is the affirmation of God as a community of persons, or *hypostaseis:*

> Previously it had been rightly asserted that God was a single *hypostasis.* But now the word was used to designate the difference. This would have done no harm if it had been asserted that the Father was a *hypostasis* and the Son and Spirit were two modes of his activity in himself and toward the world. It would have done only moderate harm if Son and Spirit had been declared *hypostaseis* in which the one Father actualized himself. . . . But by using *hypostasis* both of the Father and of the Son and Spirit, serious confusion was introduced.[31]

Cobb argues against this "mystification" as nonbiblical and "speculative," while commending our seeing the relation of Son and Spirit to Father as analogous to the relation of our thinking and feeling to ourself. He further suggests that we might understand the Spirit in its transcendent character as "the resurrection of the dead or the Kingdom of Heaven."[32] However speculative the communal understanding of the Trinity may be, Cobb is honest in pointing out that his formulations also derive in part from the speculations of Whitehead. It is clear that his interpretation of the Logos is informed by Whitehead's understanding of God's "primordial nature," while his interpretation of the Spirit corresponds to Whitehead's understanding of God's "consequent nature."[33]

The difficulty for a theology of peace in conceiving God's unity as personal in this Whiteheadian way is that it provides images and concepts suggesting that our world has greater unity with God and in itself than it really has had, and that therefore the transformation from a relatively peaceful and just past toward a more peaceful and just future may occur with much less pain and struggle than is really the case. To think of a direct movement from the Logos' eternal valuation of every possibility in God's primordial nature, through their actualization as guided by the initial aims of the Logos immanent in every event and then concretely experienced by God in his consequent nature as "the Kingdom of Heaven," is to envision the world process with a metaphysical structure that disguises most of its conflict and pain.

Cobb ends his discussion of the Trinity and his volume on Christology with the affirmation that his way of thinking is intended to be the way "the Christian understanding of the Trinity can become what it should always have been, a way of affirming our liberty in Christ."[34] There can be no objection to this fundamental concern for liberty, but it must be noted that there is no comparable concern at this point for justice, and thus little modification of liberalism's understanding of liberty by the liberation insights that have emerged in the struggles for liberty in contexts of great injustice.

Cobb's later work incorporates a more liberationist concern for liberty and justice. He supports Moltmann's formulation of theological images "in such a way as to direct Christian energies toward the liberation of the oppressed."[35] But he agrees with his fellow process theologian Schubert Ogden that Moltmann's concepts "focus on the existential meaning of God for us without dealing at all adequately with the metaphysical being of God in himself."[36] In trying again to define a concept of God that will fit the imagery of political theology and ground its existential meaning, Cobb commends once more the conceptuality found in Alfred North Whitehead's philosophy.[37] In this later work, however, he develops at greater length the understanding of redemption provided by a Whiteheadian understanding of God's "consequent nature":

> Whitehead envisions that in the divine life, far more than in the human, there is a redemption of the evil of the world, a redemption which does not remove its evil, but which includes it within a whole to which even human evil can make some positive contribution, however limited. God suffers with us, but the suffering does not destroy God as it can destroy us.[38]

This transcendental view of redemption in God's consequent nature, though perhaps ultimately true vis-à-vis any finite cosmos, suggests a dualism between the personal or hypostatic life of God and the life of God's creation that appears both to denigrate the ultimate meaning of the incarnation of the Logos and the Christian's ultimate concern for the peace of the creation. I am not suggesting that this is Cobb's intention, only that it is the subtle consequence of his interpretation of the Trinity.

The unhappy theological consequences of this transcendental metaphysics for a theology of peace may also be seen from the other end, as it were, when the focus falls on the Christian's ethical responsibility to participate in the struggle for liberation. In a word, the consequence is a tendency toward moralism. Schubert Ogden's more recent christological reflection is marked both by a concern to elaborate a liberationist Christology and by a total omission, which really amounts to a rejection, of any discussion of God's being as trinitarian.[39] Ogden understands the apostolic witness to Jesus the Christ as presenting him as "the gift and demand of God's love made fully explicit," and supports the claim that Jesus not only proclaimed "the liberating love of God and summoned his hearers to live in the freedom of God's children but himself also lived in such freedom, to the extent, indeed, of perfectly actualizing it in his own life."[40] He also understands this to be the essential meaning of Paul's Christology of the cross and resurrection, though his more or less Bultmannian hermeneutic sees Paul's Christology of the cross as requiring complete demythologization:

> This is in no way to suggest, however, that it is in terms and categories of Paul's christology of the cross that we today

should seek to develop our own christology of liberation. These terms and categories are no less mythological than those of the apocalyptic eschatology in which the earliest witness to Jesus was formulated, and we have no choice but to consistently demythologize the one as well as the other.[41]

As a demythologized metaphysical substitute for trinitarian theology, Ogden elaborates the view that God "is the strictly universal *individual* whose boundless love for all things is their sole primal source as well as their only final end."[42] This is, of course, his own restatement of Whitehead's transcendental metaphysics, although he no longer thinks it can be categoreal on the basis of metaphysical analogy. Our understanding of God as love, according to Ogden, must be understood as "symbolic" in that it refers only to human existence and relations and not to the structure of ultimate reality in itself.[43] Transcendental metaphysics in Ogden's theology may define ultimate reality only in terms of the conditions that are necessarily implied if such human love is to be possible, which at least saves theological assertions symbolically based on human love from being "only a symbol" in the pejorative sense. For Ogden's neoclassical metaphysics, the kerygmatic meaning of Jesus as the gift and demand of God's love implies the necessity of God as the "center of universal *interaction*" who both acts on and is acted upon by all things.[44]

On the basis of this non-trinitarian Christology, Ogden seeks to provide "deideologized" guidance for Christian ethical practice that distinguishes, without separating, spiritual freedom and political responsibility. Yet his accent clearly falls on the side of ethical responsibility:

> If Christian freedom means there should be justice, and hence freedom and equality, throughout society and culture, it also means that the majority who are more the victims than the agents of society's divisions have the *right* to demand such freedom and equality, even as the minority who are more the agents than the victims of the same divisions have the *responsibility* to help the majority to receive this right.[45]

Though he wants to affirm Christ as both the sacrament and the example of liberating love, his emphasis is clearly on living up to

Christ's "example" that we involve ourselves in the ongoing struggles for basic justice to "make" the point of Christology.

As excellent as this discussion is, it may be seen that Ogden's transcendental metaphysics can only interpret sacramental experience as a human individual interacting with God as the "universal individual" in a way that implies ethical responsibility for peace with justice but cannot interpret this experience as participation in the Holy Spirit of peace. His radical demythologization of the church's trinitarian tradition does not allow him theologically to affirm that ethical action for peace with justice is as such a sacramental participation in the trinitarian being of God.

This may be more clearly seen when Ogden's thought is juxtaposed with a Latin American liberation theologian like Leonardo Boff, who seeks "to rescue"—we may interpolate, in view of Ogden's thought, "from demythologization"—"the experience that underlies the New Testament statements of the Johannine school and Paul's reflections on Christ and the Spirit."[46] Boff interprets the "indwelling of the Holy Trinity" in both personal and communal terms:

> Insofar as human beings are led to open up to the mystery of themselves, they are also led by the supreme mystery to an intimate encounter with the Trinity. The generation of truth in us reflects the eternal generation of the Truth of the Father: the Son. Our love, through which we communicate with others, reflects the eternal flow of the Father's and Son's mutual love: the Holy Spirit. . . . The mystery of the Trinity is reflected in human community, which lives by truth, keeps seeking more truth, finds its nourishment in love, and works constantly for social relations based on greater love and brotherhood.[47]

This understanding of God's trinitarian being, grounded in spiritual participation in divine and human community, led Boff as he developed his Christology to ground it in God's trinitarian being:

> The structure which is contained in all creation, especially in human reality, and which achieved its maximum visibility in Jesus of Nazareth, was created as an analogy to the very structures of the mystery of the Triune God. But it was through Jesus Christ that this was revealed to human aware-

> ness in an explicit manner, not so much through words but
> in the way in which he lived his human existence—a trans-
> parent, limpid and complete openness and giving to God and
> others.[48]

The revelation in Jesus' christic existential structure of the
trinitarian structure contained in all creation leads Boff to a "sacramental" articulation of liberation Christology, in contrast to
Ogden's excessively ethical articulation.

> The real situation with all its contradiction is here perceived
> by an intuitive and sapiential process of cognition. I call it
> "sacramental" because in the facts of real life it symbolically
> intuits the presence of oppression and the urgent need for
> liberation.[49]

One might put this in Moltmann's terms as a participation in the
pathos of God's Holy Spirit, revealed in Christ's crucifixion, that
draws and leads us into genuine empathy with all who suffer,
thereby sharing the suffering of the Redeemer and the grief of the
Creator as the personal and communal motivation to enter into the
divine work of creating peace with justice.

Boff sees this sacramental participation in the redemption of
creation as leading to and requiring conversion. "Positively viewed,
conversion is the implementation of altered *relationships* at every
level of personal and social reality. These altered *relationships* will
express concrete forms of liberation and anticipate the kingdom of
God."[50] The character of these converted relationships, however,
is only fully revealed in Christ's crucifixion:

> When Jesus embraced death of his own free will [although it
> was imposed on him], he reveals the total freedom of himself
> and his projects. He points up one concrete way of fleshing
> out the reality of God's kingdom when he accepts death out
> of love, maintains his fellowship with the downtrodden of
> history, pardons those who have afflicted him, and puts him-
> self into God's hands in the face of historical failure.[51]

Christian conversion thus understood obviously entails participation in a process of conflict and struggle. But in the light of Christ's
resurrection, it is sacramental participation in such a process that
leads toward peace as the fulfillment of God's intention for the
whole creation:

> All authentically human growth, all authentic justice in so-
> cial relationships, and all real increase and growth in life
> represent a way in which the resurrection is actualized here
> and now while its future fulfillment is being prepared.[52]

Our ethical struggle for peace in a peaceless world may then be
experienced and interpreted as the gracious gift of participation in
the power and pathos of the trinitarian life of our Creator and
Redeemer.

The Universality of Peace and the Catholicity of the Church

It is now fully obvious that a theology of peace affirms the salvific
presence and action of God in the whole world. Logos Christology
within a trinitarian theology affirms salvation within, but also
beyond, the visible institutional church. When the Logos is understood as "creative transformation" in the relatively dualistic sense
of "dialectical panentheism," as developed above, Christian persons and churches are called spiritually and politically to participate in transforming the violently conflictual social reality of which
they are a part.

This commitment to the universality of peace, however, creates
a crisis for the identity of the church within and over against its
world. To the degree that there is thoroughgoing ecclesial involve-
ment in sociopolitical struggles for peace, based on the conviction
that this is to participate in God's redemption of the whole creation, the distinction between church and world becomes fluid and
perhaps flawed. If there is christological and soteriological continuity between church and world, the church properly participates in
extra-ecclesial political processes and the ideologies that interpret
and support them. But when the church crosses its institutional
boundaries to serve what may be salvific political processes toward
peace, it also runs the risk of ideologically compromising its identity as given by the Logos' particular incarnation in Jesus the
Christ. For every ideational and social process in a fallen world is
subject to the distortion of sin.

Because working toward peace requires this risk, the theology of
peace must be equally concerned to maintain the church's authentic catholic identity. As the early church sought to define itself

within and over against the Roman Empire, it characterized itself in the Nicene Creed as "one holy catholic and apostolic Church." Without repudiating these "marks," the Reformation churches stressed the criteria of the "word truly preached" and the "sacraments rightly administered." These criteria can be deeply misleading if they are thought of as abstract essences defining a purely spiritual church, but they are useful if it is remembered that the churches are concrete human communities responding to God's gracious action in Jesus Christ for the redemption of the whole creation of which they are a part. The churches must remember that they are on the human side of the Creator-creature distinction, characterized by processes common to all human communities and institutions and shaped by the cultures of the social groups they comprise.

The full recognition of the churches as human communities means that these ecclesial criteria must be interpreted and applied "non-docetically." Just as there is no place in a theology of peace for a docetic Christology that rejects the full, Jewish, vulnerable, creative humanity of Jesus, so too is there no place for a docetic ecclesiology that refuses to recognize the church in all of its many-faceted human, social, political, economic, and cultural dimensions. Given this recognition, however, the Nicene and Reformation characteristics may be understood as criteria for measuring processes and practices essential for constituting and expressing spiritual communities responding to Jesus as the Christ.

The unity and universality of such communities is constituted by the Holy Spirit guiding their response to the revelation they have received in Jesus. The complete, concrete image mediated by the memory in the canonical Gospels of his life, teaching, death, and resurrection and the kerygmatic interpretations of Jesus mediated by the New Testament and the churches' traditions guide the churches' faith in one God transforming their communities toward love for all neighbors. Thus the church can only be and become the church as it receives the gift of reconciliation across all gender distinctions, class stratifications, ideological conflicts, and racial and national divisions.

Whatever unity is actualized in and through the whole of humanity, however, will remain fragmentary and incomplete. To be "catholic" is to become *kata holos,* through the whole. All concretely human becoming whole, however, is mediated through the partiality of those parts of fragmented humanity to which we are actually related. It is God alone who has the power to constitute the whole and reconstitute it as whole despite all divisive alienations. The church's catholicity as a fully human unity and universality is always provisional and proleptic as it participates in what God has given and gives in the hope that it will be eschatologically fulfilled. But the "always already" of its penultimate catholicity is also always oriented by the "not yet" of its continuing fragmentation toward a fulfillment that remains eschatological promise. Susan Thistlethwaite, with insights gained through feminist struggles in the church, argues for adequate recognition of our "messy, conflictual, and many-faceted historical reality":

> One must move through the conflictual, divided character of experience and not skip over it. A too quick jump to unity is frequently achieved by asserting the experience of the dominant group in society as a universal.[53]

The ecumenical church has tested its fragile catholicity as it has sought to enter more fully into the contemporary struggles for peace and justice. Perhaps the controversy has nowhere been more fierce than in the Programme to Combat Racism of the World Council of Churches since it began in 1969. At the beginning, as so often is the case, there was a certain naïveté. It was noted in the report of the Working Group on Racism and Theology in the consultation called in 1980 to deal with the controversies that had emerged because of grants to liberation movements especially in Southern Africa:

> At the beginning of ecumenical debate about racism it was widely believed in the ecumenical movement "that by preaching the brotherhood of man and by the spreading of modern education, race prejudice would soon be eliminated." . . . The churches did not take seriously the "non-rational" character of overt and covert racism, and the influence of political and economic factors on racial discrimination. Instead they believed that the classical doctrines of the Christian faith were a sufficient guide for the work of the ecumenical movement in overcoming racial discrimination.[54]

These "classical doctrines," of course, remained in some ways necessary for their catholic action but not sufficient for contemporary actualization. Radical repentance and creative transformation were required in a way that stretched and enlarged the church's catholicity:

> Reconciliation between peoples, nations and cultures demands repentance—radical changes of attitudes and sacrificial action. We have learnt to appreciate this anew—and to express solidarity with the oppressed. Thus combating racism is a significant contribution to the search for both the unity of the Church and human kind.[55]

It was and is precisely at the point of the relation of justice to peace that this controversy remains in some ways unresolved: that is, over the issue of violence in liberation struggles. No matter how "one-sided" this concern for violence may seem on the part of privileged Europeans and North Americans, it remains a proper and even crucial concern for the church catholic.[56] But old "unities" achieved through a consensus of the privileged must now be reopened and extended by perspectives that come from "the underside of history." The whole methodology of the ecumenical movement as it continues to struggle toward catholicity has been challenged and transformed through recognition of the "essential *contextuality* of theology."[57] That is to say, there is no privileged position from which the authentically universal may be discerned and defined, so it is especially necessary in a conflicted world to give at least a preliminary privilege to those who hitherto have been marginalized and rendered voiceless, so that the church universal may increasingly become *kata holos.*

Exactly the same issue has more recently become notorious in the concern of the Vatican to limit, if not silence, the theological expression of Roman Catholic liberation theologies in South America. Leonardo Boff's analysis of the relation liberation theology has to the institutional church in his *Church: Charism and Power* has focused this controversy in the church catholic.[58] Basing his theology on the New Testament teaching concerning charisms in 1 Corinthians, Ephesians, and Romans, he affirms that every Christian—including the peasants and workers in Latin American Base Communities—have gifts of ministry that dare not be repressed.[59] To allow the church to be structured through the full diversity of the charisms given by the Holy Spirit will renew and extend its catholicity.

> At the very least, it will foster a spirit, which in the strength of the Holy Spirit, will revitalize the traditional and hierarchical institutions of the Church. And the history of salvation tells us that where the Spirit is active, we can count on the unexpected, the new that has not yet been seen.[60]

All this means that a theology of peace, precisely because it is committed to the criterion of catholicity, must tolerate a degree of ambiguity that has not always been accepted by those who fail to recognize not only how pluralistic but how conflicted our world really is. David Tracy's theological work has made an important contribution to compelling recognition of pluralistic ambiguity as we move again toward a public theology based on interpretation of our religious classics. Though agreeing with Northrop Frye that the scriptures have served "as a kind of great code for Western culture," he stresses the "extraordinary flexibility" with which they have so functioned.[61] He argues that the ecumenical church must use both the hermeneutics of retrieval and the hermeneutics of suspicion if its catholicity is to be marked not only by our apostolic tradition but also by the creative transformation to which it witnesses:

> Whitehead once suggested that a religious sensibility begins with a sense that "something is awry." In ways that Whitehead could not have foreseen, we now sense that something may be very awry indeed in all our classics and traditions, including the religious ones. No great religion should hesitate to apply to itself its own suspicion of either sin or ignorance. As surely as there are religious hermeneutics of retrieval, there are also religious hermeneutics of suspicion to uncover what may be awry in the religion itself.[62]

When we follow strategies of both retrieval and suspicion, we seek both to ground ourselves in the church's apostolic recognition of the gracious Word incarnate in Jesus and to open ourselves to the Logos' continuing redemptive transformation of our reality. This means opening ourselves to the conflict that liberationist perspectives from third world, black, and feminist Christians necessarily bring to the interpretation of that tradition. Because none of these conflicts are easily resolved, they require exactly the trust that a community grounded in the grace revealed in Jesus provides, so we may risk ourselves in the mutual critique that engenders a dynamic catholicity in the movement toward peace.

The increasingly transformationist positions taken by dimensions of the church, such as the U.S. Catholic bishops and the United Methodist bishops in their pastoral letters on peace, have had ambiguous effects in the congregations addressed. Many local leaders continue to avoid the controversial issues of peace for fear of congregational conflict or anticipation of apathetic responses that will only increase the psychic numbing of hopelessness. But increasingly wise methods are being developed to move congregations beyond anger and apathy toward "Peacemaking Without Division."[63] Individualistic and rationalistic argumentation in a win-lose context is transformed through processes that deal honestly with feelings and personal stories in a context of conflict management using a win-win paradigm.

It must be recognized, however, that conflict management does not usually yield conflict resolution. Kenneth Boulding, one of the pioneers in this field, notes that we seldom totally resolve conflict: "Rather it is more like a dance where we learn not to step on each other's feet; we don't ever totally resolve the issues, but we do learn to manage the dance more gracefully."[64] Christian congregations under skilled leadership may become such graceful communities, where the difficult issues of peace with justice may be dealt with in a way that enhances the genuine catholicity of Christ's church. The danger of division may become the mutual necessity of repentance and transformation in a graciously dynamic community.

David Tracy's eloquence has stated our conclusion concerning the church's dynamic catholicity as it engages in the struggle for peace:

> There is no release for any of us from the conflict of interpretation if we would understand at all. The alternative is not an escape into the transient pleasures of irony or a flight into despair and cynicism. The alternative is not a new kind of innocence or passivity masking apathy. Whoever fights for hope, fights on behalf of us all. Whoever acts on that hope, acts in a manner worthy of a human being. And whoever so

acts, I believe, acts in a manner faintly suggestive of the
reality and power of that God in whose image human beings
were formed to resist, to think, and to act. The rest is prayer,
observance, discipline, conversation, and actions of solidar-
ity-in-hope. Or the rest is silence.[65]

The rest, of course, dare not be silence. Our silence may be broken
as we participate in Christ's dynamic unity of creative transformation in Christian ecclesial communities that sacramentally participate in the power and pathos of the trinitarian relationality of God
and thus move toward the universality of peace.

6

The Universal Church and the Praxis of Peace

The biblical understanding of peace I have been describing, as the wholeness of personal integrity and social communion in all of humanity *(shalom),* also affirms that such personal-social wholeness is possible only in covenant relation with God, who, as the universal Creator and Redeemer of all being, embraces the whole and makes it whole. Though the more fortunate of us human beings move through early familial and neighborhood forms of community toward experiences of national (and even approximations of worldwide) human community, the finitude of our cultures and the sinful alienation of our divisions have made our experience of such wholeness fragmentary and elusive. Thus Christian faith and hope has come to understand personal and social peace as the eschatological telos of the creative process in which we now live, and to interpret our present limited experience of peace as participation in the Holy Spirit, revealed in Christ's resurrection as the loving, suffering relationality of God.

Theological Recapitulation

In more abstract theological formulations, the Christian experience of peace in continuing struggle with the limits and conflicts of history has led to an understanding of "dialectical peace" within a history understood through "relative dualism" as marred by demonic forces of bondage and destruction. Our saving relation to the crucified and resurrected Christ in the Holy Spirit, under the historical conditions of relative dualism, is best interpreted through the concept of "dialectical panentheism," where the historical suffering of a fallen creation is understood as taken into God's relational being to be transformed by God's suffering and victorious love.

Faithful response to the crucified and risen Christ enables renewed participation in the creative Spirit of God. Expressed in more concrete terms, whatever our personal histories of limitation and failure, however deep the alienation from our existential springs of life in family and culture, no matter how tragically wounded or possessed by society's demonic structures, we Christians may receive through Christ the Holy Spirit that engenders, empowers, and finally fulfills life. We are thus enabled again to integrate the various dimensions of our being in self-actualization and social interaction in our world. Because Jesus' spirit could not finally be destroyed by the demonic forces that crucified him, we Christians live with renewed confidence in our ability to interact with our world so as to transform it, even as we are being transformed. When God's perfect love revealed in Christ overcomes our fear, we again accept our participatory relation with our world and become what we are created to be—spiritual centers of social relation, despite the suffering that such social vulnerability entails. To enter into renewed relation with God, whose very being is constituted relationally as Father, Son, and Spirit, is to know the ultimate basis for the divine image in ourselves as the communal image of our peaceful relation with the whole world.

The experience of Christian salvation as peace, therefore, may be realized, celebrated, and practiced only in community. Yet none of our concrete communities, including our churches, even approximate universal community. We may know the creator God at work through one Logos to bring the whole creation to communion in one Spirit only in sacramental community: that is, in a community that knows it is constituted by its participation in God and thus remains open to the relational universal that transcends it. On the basis of this understanding, minuscule Christian communities in the first century became witnesses to God's universal peace within and against the Roman Empire. The "Epistle to Diognetus" vividly described the social form of this sacramental participation in the early church:

The distinction between Christians and other men is neither in country nor language nor customs. For they do not dwell in cities in some place of their own, nor do they use any strange variety of dialect, nor practice an extraordinary kind of life. . . . Yet while living in Greek and barbarian cities, according as each obtained his lot, and following the local customs, both in clothing and food and in the rest of life, they show forth the wonderfully and confessedly strange character of the constitution of their own citizenship. They dwell in their own fatherlands, but as if sojourners in them; they share all things as citizens, and suffer all things as strangers. Every foreign country is their fatherland, and every fatherland is a foreign country.[1]

When their social relations are sacramentally understood and practiced, Christians participate in their concrete communities as grounded in the creative and redemptive God, while not claiming triumphally that any of their communities has complete unity with God nor seeking faithlessly to escape the suffering and struggle necessary to move them toward universal peace. A sacramental understanding of our spiritual participation in the divine trinitarian and human social communities enables us to experience and interpret the ongoing struggle for peace with justice in our world as the gracious gift of participation in the power and pathos of the Spirit of our Creator and Redeemer. The unity and universality of the church in the midst of our national, racial, sexual, and class struggles is constituted only by the Holy Spirit, who guides us in our response to the revelation of God's universal Logos revealed in Jesus for the continuing redemptive transformation of our communities.

The Meaning of Praxis

It is obvious that, within so dynamic, social, and eschatological a theology, peace may not be understood as a particular state of affairs but as a peculiar process of acting—and interacting. It is not so much some*thing* as something *done*—together. Peace is thus not to be understood as the tranquility of order but as the activity of ordering nontranquil selves and societies. That is, peace is the *praxis* of peace. Or, as the aphorism of the Fellowship of Reconciliation puts it, There is no way to peace; peace is the way.[2]

The term "praxis" returned to Christian vocabularies because the usual understanding of the more widely used cognate term "practice" no longer connotes what must now be understood. Though suspect in some theological circles because it comes to many of us via liberation theology from Marx and Hegel, praxis has a straightforward meaning that has far more to do with a critique of the dominant understanding of subject-object relations in our scientific culture than it has with the critique of capitalism in our political economy.[3] Practice has come to mean the rational use of means that are externally related to, but instrumental in the attainment of, a desired end. Praxis, in contrast, is seen as a dialectical process of internally related events from which a result emerges. The means and the end are internally related.

When peace *practice* is understood in the more usual way, peace may be conceived as a state of affairs that the practice of diplomacy or deterrence or perhaps even warfare is meant to achieve, for the means are external and instrumental to the end. In such circumstances, even a strategic missile with ten atomic warheads may be named the "peacekeeper." Practices governed by this view have led to various forms of manipulated, imposed, and imperialistic peace that are often hard to distinguish from the conflicts they supposedly resolved. Given the finite and ideological character of all of our preconceptions of peace, any peace achieved through such practices almost inevitably becomes a German, or a Communist, or a Muslim, or a democratic "peace."

A more genuine peace is always a dynamic emergent from a dialogical and dialectical process. Praxis is the cultivation of those shared practices that allow such a peace to emerge, not according to the preconception of the more powerful, clever, or unscrupulous participants but through a process of struggle, negotiation, and dialogue leading toward a genuinely voluntary consensus, no matter how fragile and temporary it may be. The fragile and temporary character of consensual peace, indeed, serves to underscore that it is achieved and maintained only by the continuous praxis of peace in a dynamic and open human process.

Gray Cox has analyzed three traditions of the praxis of peace, differentiated by the degree of alienation and conflict that divides the participants: the Quaker process of consensus, the Harvard Law School's Negotiation Project, and the Gandhian practice of satyagraha.[4] The Quakers share a common religious faith that enables them more readily to deal with the existential alienations of their personal individuation; the Harvard Negotiation Project deals with people and communities with different value systems but a willingness to communicate; while Gandhian satyagraha found a nonviolent way to communicate and finally to negotiate with the hostile and oppressive representatives of a colonial government ready to use violence.

The Quaker *consensual praxis* has five stages or levels: quieting impulses, addressing concerns, gathering consensus, finding clearness, and bearing witness. This process works best where the persons involved are already peaceably committed to arriving at communal decisions that will move them toward a more universal peace with justice.

The Harvard Law School's *negotiating praxis* is designed for those who are not yet as peaceable as Quakers intend to be. Here the attempt is to move the participants from the practice of positional bargaining to the praxis of "principled negotiation."[5] This requires a search for shared interests behind conflicting positions, the inventing of options for mutual gain, and the devising of objectively fair procedures for arriving at agreement.

Gandhi's *struggling praxis* of nonviolent satyagraha was devised to deal with the unpeaceful who consider themselves so powerful that they need not be concerned about shared interests, mutual gain, or fair procedures. Here the process must begin with the self-liberation of the oppressed by their learning a self-disciplined autonomy. The poor and marginalized must be liberated to act freely without "attachment" to the promises or threats that beset them. When their action is genuinely free, their various forms of noncooperation or civil disobedience are not aimed so much to coerce the compliance of the powerful as to "melt their hearts" by showing them the power of the moral truth that enables self-suffering. Gandhi invented the term "satyagraha" from *satya* (truth) and *agraha* (firmness) as a synonym for force and translated it as "truth force," or sometimes as "love force" or "soul force." It is a praxis for the most alienated and conflicted situations, where one side must take upon itself a suffering that "forces" alienated opponents, who are yet believed to share in humanity's image of God, to see the truth and finally move toward a more universal peace with justice.

The fact that a Gandhian form of struggling praxis makes use of force, albeit "soul force," requires it to be measured by the criteria of justice just as any other mode of force. When Christians must move beyond consensual and negotiating praxis to the use of their own kind of force in a "world in which interest is set against interest and force against force," as Reinhold Niebuhr characteristically put it,[6] then the discriminate moral judgments of critical faculties developed in honest dialogue must be added to the religious impulses of loving nonviolence. Niebuhr is certainly correct in his rejection of any dualism that would identify "soul force" with nonegoistic motives and "body force" with egoistic ones, and in his judgment that "one man [sic] may keep another enslaved purely by 'soul' force."[7]

It is equally important to note, however, that this astute critic of pragmatic pacifism was most acutely critical of those with great economic and other forms of covert power who arbitrarily insist on the "love absolutism of the gospels" only when their interests are threatened. What Niebuhr called the "unconscious class prejudice" of the middle-class church does not afflict to the same degree the social movements of the poor and marginalized who have provided us the best paradigms of the Gandhian form of struggling praxis.[8] The later Niebuhr also revised what he characterized as his earlier "rather violent, and sometimes extravagant, reaction to what [he] defined as 'utopianism.' "[9] My perspective is in some ways an extension of this revision begun by Niebuhr, who was one of my most influential teachers twenty-five years ago. The "universal community" he discerned as emerging then has grown both as spiritual possibility and moral necessity now.[10]

Since this is not a book of techniques, these brief descriptions of various forms of peace praxis must suffice.[11] They indicate the possibility of a family of practices that fit a church that understands itself as a locus for sacramental participation in the Holy Spirit's work of bringing God's creation to universal peace. We must now turn to a more extended discussion of the emerging peace praxis of the universal church.

The Emergence of the Universal Church

The emergence and institutionalization of the ecumenical church has been one of the most important developments for Protestant and Orthodox Christians in the twentieth century. Motivated by the internal dynamic of their own faith and enabled by modern technologies that make rapid communication and travel possible, this churchly movement toward unity was also required by the worldwide dimensions of the devastating conflicts that modern civilization had spawned. Working for Indian liberation between the two World Wars that European societies had fought during our century, Gandhi wrote, "Civilization is not an incurable disease, but it should never be forgotten that the English people are at present afflicted by it."[12] The churches within the European civilization afflicted by such devastating alienation also began to take a new ecumenical responsibility for international peace in the Stockholm Conference of 1925 and the Oxford Conference of 1937 sponsored by the Life and Work Movement, which later entered the World Council of Churches when it was constituted in Amsterdam in 1948.

World War II had blocked the creation of any ecumenical structures through which the churches might take responsibility for international peace. But following the devastation of that conflict, the churches moved quickly in a conference in Cambridge, England, in 1946 to plan for what became the Commission of the Churches on International Affairs (CCIA) within the World Council of Churches in 1948. When members of the Council of the Evangelical Church in Germany met representatives of the World Council of Churches (in formation) in Stuttgart on October 19, 1945, they had said:

> We are not only conscious of oneness with our nation in a great community of sufferings, but also in a solidarity of guilt. With great pain we say: Unending suffering has been brought by us to many people and countries. . . . We accuse ourselves that we did not witness more courageously, pray more faithfully, believe more joyously, love more ardently. . . . We hope in God that through the joint service of the churches, the spirit of violence and revenge that begins again today to

become powerful may be controlled, and the spirit of peace
and love come to command, in which alone tortured humanity can find healing.

During the last forty years more than three hundred churches
from around the world have been responding to those who have
suffered the consequences of idolatrous states seeking superpower
status, so that "through the joint service of the churches . . .
tortured humanity can find healing." The constitution of the
World Council of Churches defines, as one of its crucial functions,
"To express the common concern of the churches in the service of
human need, the breaking down of barriers between people, and
the promotion of the human family in justice and peace."

Decades of effort to achieve and express worldwide "common
concern," however, have also illumined the immense difficulties in
doing so. After reviewing the contemporary peace witness of the
churches in East and West during the 1980s, I concluded:

> Whatever else has been accomplished in these four decades
> of ecumenical work—and it has been considerable—the
> problem of the universal and the particular has been con-
> cretely reestablished in the life of the churches. Striving for
> some "universal" peace and/or justice becomes formal and
> empty when disengaged from the very concrete political,
> economic and social dynamics of particular congregations in
> nations having a social history uniquely their own.[13]

The World Council of Churches has had to wrestle with how
their concern for the universal affects the particular church-state
relations of its member churches. Churches who covenant together
in worldwide community now must take three hundred other
churches from every continent into account as they interact with
their states' policies and programs. They must take their obligations to international community just as seriously as they take their
obligations to the communities of the particular states in which
they live and bear witness. In a consultation held in 1976 to study
these issues, fifty representatives reflected on the dynamic paradox
their churches were facing:

> There is in the world today a strong tension, often a conflict
> between universal and particular perspectives. In the course
> of the last centuries and decades, the world has been drawn

more and more by scientific, technological, economic and political developments into one system. . . . It is becoming less and less possible to respond both to God's promise and the power which threatens the future on less than an international scale. . . . Though drawn into one system, the world is as sharply if not more sharply divided than ever before. . . . There is not yet genuine interdependence among the nations. Their relations are distorted by political and ideological domination, economic exploitation, social discrimination, etc.[14]

The paradox of being drawn into a universal system while remaining sharply divided may be understood better by using the distinction between external and internal relations we developed in our discussion of the difference between practice and praxis. The international system thus far is very largely built up by the practice of external relations. Its sharp divisions remain because there has thus far been too little praxis of internal relations. This kind of contradiction between external and internal relations is dangerously explosive. To be externally interdependent without being internally interrelated is almost a sure formula for increasing conflict. Where there is no genuinely open dialogue, we are left to increase our deterrence of the ever closer opponent and strengthen our positional bargaining stance within an ever more interdependent system. This is exactly the contemporary situation of national-security states trying to maintain "peace through strength" by nuclear deterrence.

Responding to exactly this kind of world situation, the General Assembly of the World Council of Churches in Vancouver in 1983 said, "The biblical vision of peace with justice for all, of wholeness of unity of all God's people, is not one of several options for followers of Christ. It is an imperative in our time."[15] In responding to this contemporary imperative, however, the World Council must use the dialogical channels available to it, while helping expand them toward new possibilities. This means it must work through a network of churches whose historical identity is defined in part through their relation with a particular nation:

Its member churches live and witness in a wide variety of social, economic, political and ideological situations. Their possibilities of action and the problems they face differ widely. History, tradition, culture and the present circumstances all have a bearing on these. Public actions of the WCC will have to take into account these factors and should be characterized by a sensitivity to the special needs of each church and national situation.[16]

The particular national identities of the constituent churches, however, are being continually stretched toward the universal. The Oxford Conference of 1937 and, to a lesser extent, the Amsterdam Assembly of 1948 were still dominated by the anxieties and hopes of the churches in Europe (mostly Western Europe at that) and North America. European culture's terrible "time of troubles," revealed in their two World Wars, had brought their historic churches beyond their nationalism only that far. But by the time of the Geneva Conference on Church and Society in 1966, the conciliar dialogue of the churches had come to include the hopes and anxieties of the churches in Africa, Asia, and Latin America. This has led to an increasing emphasis on a "Gospel-based bias towards the poor and oppressed" found mainly in these so-called "third world" nations.[17] This concern for the poor and oppressed has been complicated for "first world" churches by the entrance of "second world" Russian and other Eastern European churches into this conciliar process after the Delhi Assembly in 1961, because now this ecumenical concern could be interpreted as under the influence of Marxism. These differentiations of first, second, and third within the one world of God's creation indicate the continuing division and tensions the churches must face and overcome as they develop a peace praxis of internal relations stretching toward the universal. The continuing alienations between democratic capitalist, communist, and liberationist blocs continues to affect, and even infect, the churches as they participate in the power and pathos of God's universal relationality.

Mainline North American Churches
Within the Universal Church

The entrance of North American churches into the World Council of Churches in 1948 coincided with the beginning of the so-called "cold war." Struck for the first time in our national history with the menace of total war by the Japanese attack on Pearl Harbor in 1941, and frightened by the unresolved conflicts of World War II, from which the Soviet Union had also emerged a victor, American national policy began "a search for security that has dominated national politics in our time."[18] It led for the first time in our history to peacetime conscription in 1948, when eighty-one more congressional representatives voted for it than had voted for conscription in 1940 when we were facing World War II. The Truman Doctrine of the containment of communism led to the formation of the National Security Council, the global development of the Central Intelligence Agency, and military alliances such as the North Atlantic Treaty Organization (NATO). The often unsubstantiated charges of the House Un-American Activities Committee and Senator Joseph McCarthy expanded the fear of Communist subversion within American society, so that much of governmental activity was and still is shielded from public examination by being classified as secret.

This mind-set is all the more dangerous in a nuclear age when these policies of national security are implemented by weapons whose scope of destruction goes far beyond anything humanity has experienced in its long history of warfare. When some of the scientists who were developing these weapons began to have doubts about the wisdom of their continuing production, they were told, as was J. Robert Oppenheimer by the Personnel Security Board, "There can be no tampering with the national security, which in times of peril must be absolute. . . . Any doubts whatsoever must be resolved in the interests of national security."[19]

It was in this national-security ethos that North American churches had to begin to find their way into the international dialogue and conciliar process of the World Council of Churches. In the very year the WCC was founded, the House Un-American Activities Committee called the Methodist Federation for Social Action a "tool of the Communist Party." Though HUAC and Senator McCarthy were finally discredited, it took the churches great effort over several decades to move from preoccupation with the threat of communism, and thus qualified support of their state's national-security policies, to a principal focus on universal peace and the redefinition of American foreign policies implied. A representative example is the movement of the Presbyterian Church in the United States (PCUS), whose General Assembly in 1954 approved a paper on "The Christian Faith and Communism" that stated, "It has become increasingly clear that the goal of communism is world domination. No one of us should be so naïve as to suppose that anything short of such a goal fits into the pattern of this atheistic philosophy."[20] By 1981, however, The United Presbyterian Church U.S.A. adopted a statement on "Peacemaking: The Believers' Calling," that took a far different position:

> Instead of concentrating exclusively on interest, security, and power, Christians should move, and urge the nation to move, to consideration of justice, freedom, and compassionate order. In such a mode, understandings of interest, security, and power are transformed and a new basis is established for United States foreign policy. . . . We must learn to relate constructively to the ground swell around the world that demands justice, seeks freedom, and aspires to conditions of community made possible by compassionate means of maintaining order.[21]

The experience of the United Methodist Church during the decade of the 1970s provides another telling illustration of the struggle which such changes in perspective required of the churches. The United Methodist General Council on Ministries, through a comprehensive process of one hundred "hearings" across the whole nation in 1970, determined that the three priority concerns of its members were: (1) resolving ethnic conflict; (2) working for world peace; and (3) averting the danger of nuclear extinction of human life. On the basis of these findings, the General Conference of 1972 adopted a denominational program on "The Bishops' Call for Peace and Self-Development of Peoples." It joined a growing concern for arms control and disarmament with the more universal form of concern for "ethnic conflict" that was being articulated in the liberation perspectives emerging in the third world. The introduction of these "foreign" analyses of the problem of racial and economic justice caused such tension and disagreement in United Methodist conferences and congregations, however, that when another grass-roots survey was taken in 1976 it was found that the highest priority was now "a recovery of the sense of personal concern for all members of the church despite profound differences of opinion." The church's concern to advance the universal conciliar process for peace and justice through its American congregations so disturbed the internal community of those congregations that many United Methodists feared their denominational name was becoming an oxymoron and opted for restoring peace and unity—at least in the church.

Struggles like these in the decades since North American churches have begun participating in the more universal conciliar process for peace have required a more careful recognition of the way in which the church is a community of communities: congregations that are focused on ministries to persons, families, and neighborhoods; denominations maintaining programs of evangelism, education, health care, and the like; national councils of churches oriented to the "common good" of their nation-states; and the ecumenical church as a universal conciliar reality.[22] The congregations and denominations in the United States are further differentiated into approximately 25 percent mainline Protestants affiliated with the National Council of Churches, 25 percent Roman Catholic, 30 percent evangelical Protestants often affiliated with the National Association of Evangelicals, 10 percent black Protestants, and 2.5 percent Jewish, leaving about 7.5 percent with no religious preference.[23]

There are pronounced differences in the political tendencies of these religious groups revealed in the research of the National Opinion Research Center.[24] Jewish believers and black Protestants defined themselves as predominantly liberal and associated with the Democratic party. Roman Catholics to a lesser degree, mainline Protestants, and evangelical Protestants to a greater degree, saw themselves as more conservative; though only mainline Protestants indicated a larger affiliation with the Republican party. At least through 1984, evangelical Protestants were divided approximately 40 percent Democratic and 30 percent Republican, while mainline Protestants were just the reverse, 40 percent Republican and 30 percent Democratic—with about 30 percent characterizing themselves as Independents in each case. This party affiliation obtained even though evangelical Protestants saw themselves as more conservative than liberal by 24 percent, while mainline Protestants were only 16 percent more conservative.

Since it is largely the mainline Protestant churches who are the participants in the ecumenical conciliar process through the WCC that we have been analyzing, it is of great interest that more of their members understand themselves as conservative than liberal and that they alone, of all the religious preferences in the United States, show a larger affiliation with the Republican party. It is this party that has remained more representative of the established political-economic ideology and economic classes in this country, while the Democratic party has increasingly become a coalition of interest groups who understand themselves as seeking justice for labor unions, racial and ethnic minorities, and so on through various programs of social change. Given the lack of political coherence in the platforms and programs of our broad two-party system, one cannot generalize very accurately about these party differences, but it is obvious that religious groups like black Protestants and Jews, whose social histories have predisposed them to concerns for some forms of justice, have very largely turned to the Democratic party as the political vehicle for such concerns. The same has been true for peace groups like the "freeze voters" of the National Freeze Campaign, who endorsed Walter Mondale's candidacy for president in 1984.

This support of the Democratic party as the political vehicle for peace-and-justice concerns is not because of some absolute or religious commitment to that party as such but because it appears to be the political process presently more open to being influenced by such concerns. This has meant for the mainline Protestant churches, influenced by the universal peace-and-justice concerns of the ecumenical conciliar process, however, that they are turned toward a political party with which their members traditionally have not had a majority affiliation. The result has been the increase of tension in the congregations that we have seen illustrated above in the Presbyterian and United Methodist churches. When these churches seek to foster political commitment on a religious basis for nuclear disarmament and third world liberation-and-justice concerns, they risk endangering, in the short term at least, the social and economic support required for their total programs of evangelism and pastoral care.

This tension is illumined when the variable of education is introduced to the analysis of religious and political preference, as Kenneth Wald's analysis indicates:

> For some groups—most clearly white Protestants from both mainline and evangelical denominations—gains in education were clearly associated with movement toward Republicanism. Most white Protestants with low levels of education were Democrats, but a plurality of those Protestants with some postsecondary schooling were Republicans.[25]

In the data from the General Social Surveys of 1980–84, 15 percent more mainline Protestants with low education were Democrats than Republicans, while approximately 25 percent more of those with higher education were in the Republican party than in the Democratic party.[26] This means that precisely those with higher social status in the leadership levels of both the society and the churches' laity were less likely to be open to the religiously based political commitments of their churches as they were influenced by the ecumenical conciliar process toward universal peace and justice.

The tension between high-social-status lay leaders and the ordained leadership of the mainline Protestant churches has also increased because the clergy of these churches have been largely educated in ecumenically oriented seminaries whose theological formulations and socioethical analyses have been increasingly influenced by the ecumenical conciliar process. This has meant that higher education for the clergy in increasingly ecumenical churches has moved them in one direction, while higher education for the laity in the nation's universities has moved them in the opposite direction.

Evangelical North American Churches and the Universal Church

What is now called evangelical Protestantism, except for its premillennial apocalypticism, was the majority theology of the so-called mainline Protestant churches in the nineteenth century and an animating force in American political life until World War

I. By that time, however, the theological challenge of biblical criticism, which required a new integration of theology and the relativities of the historical process, and the social challenges of rapid urbanization, especially in the North, where the ethos of small-town culture was increasingly displaced, began to lead to its reformulation religiously and decline politically.

Religiously, the mainline churches increasingly understood their theology as expressing more universally human values to be actualized through full participation in the relativities of a pluralistic society and world, which came to be decried by the evangelicals as too great a compromise with "secular humanism." The mainline churches saw their revisionist theologies as necessary to comprehend anew their traditional monotheistic faith in one Creator and Redeemer in a world that no longer could be understood through religious, racial, national, or class dualisms. God as revealed in Christ, they concluded, must be understood anew as present and working in biblical and ecclesial history in ways that are analogous to God's presence and activity in universal history. Evangelicals, on the other hand, sought to maintain the revelational claims for their particular history by absolutizing the verbal plenary inspiration of their inerrant Bible.

Politically, evangelicals could find no one who could embody their causes on a national level, as William Jennings Bryan had done before World War I, until Ronald Reagan almost seven decades later. Maintaining themselves primarily in the Southern United States, evangelicals chose for two generations to remain largely outside the national political arena. The Reverend Jerry Falwell, criticizing mainline Protestant clergy active in the civil rights movement in 1965, expressed their majority attitude clearly:

> Believing in the Bible as I do, I would find it impossible to stop preaching the pure saving Gospel of Jesus Christ, and begin doing anything else—including fighting communism, or participating in civil rights reforms. . . . Preachers are not called to be politicians but to be soul winners.[27]

Evangelicals, however, had begun to come back into the national political arena in 1960 when the Democratic party risked for the first time nominating a Roman Catholic, John F. Kennedy, for the presidency. Many of them objected strenuously and politically.

Some turned to support Richard Nixon, as symbolized by the public identification of their premier evangelist, Billy Graham, with Nixon's campaigns and presidency until the Watergate scandal revealed not only his political but his personal impieties. Jimmy Carter, however, moderated the extremist image of evangelicalism while genuinely representing some of its virtues. As a clearly identified evangelical Protestant, Carter received the same percentage of black and Jewish votes as Lyndon Johnson and Hubert Humphrey—or even larger—because he was seen as continuing their support for social justice, though he actually lost a majority of his fellow white Southerners to the Republican candidate.[28]

It was not, however, until the candidacies and presidency of Ronald Reagan that evangelical Protestants came fully and in some ways triumphantly back into national American politics. Reagan knew in his own familial history the pluralistic dynamics of American society as the son of a Roman Catholic father and a mother who was an enthusiastic evangelical in the Disciples of Christ church. Ronald Reagan was baptized by immersion on the basis of his personal faith at age eleven, becoming an active member in the church where his mother was a pillar; and he extended his formation in this church by completing his higher education in one of its colleges. This early background has given the later Reagan ease and familiarity in dealing with contemporary political evangelicals.[29]

By 1979, Jerry Falwell and many other evangelical Protestants had changed their minds and founded several new political-action organizations, the most prominent of which was the Moral Majority. This very name indicates their judgment that with Ronald Reagan they had finally found a candidate who might again win national majority support for their political program. They articulated this program in a "Christian Bill of Rights," which, in addition to stressing their opposition to abortion and their support for such causes as voluntary prayer and Bible reading in public schools, specifically joined moral and military strength in its Amendment VIII:

> We believe in the right to expect our national leaders to keep this country morally and militarily strong so that the religious freedom and Gospel preaching might continue unhindered. [I Peter 2:13-17][30]

On this basis they joined secular political conservatives in supporting increased domestic military spending and "anticommunist"
movements around the globe, including the governments of Chile,
El Salvador, Guatemala, Israel, Honduras, and South Africa, and
the "freedom fighters" in Afghanistan, Angola, Mozambique, and
Nicaragua.

Ronald Reagan was their candidate of choice over two other
evangelical Protestants, Jimmy Carter and John Anderson, because only he fully endorsed their political program. Though some
felt he had not pushed their "pro-family" agenda hard enough in
his first term, no one could complain that he had not fully enacted
their military and anticommunist agenda, so they supported his
reelection in 1984 with new enthusiasm. It was on these military
issues above all that the alliance of the Reagan administration and
the evangelical Protestant right wing contradicted the political
wisdom of the mainline churches' growing commitment to at least
nuclear disarmament on the basis of a negotiated reconciliation
with the Soviet Union.

The political judgment of the evangelical right wing about the
necessity of military confrontation with the Soviet Union and its
allies is informed and undergirded by an apocalyptic premillennial
theology. Evangelical Protestantism moved from the millennial
optimism of Jonathan Edwards in the eighteenth century, and the
postmillennial social activism of Francis Asbury and Charles Fin-
ney in the nineteenth century, to the premillennial pessimism of
Dwight L. Moody, Billy Sunday, and the Niagara Bible Conference at the end of the nineteenth century. Here they followed the
premillennial moves of the more sectarian Seventh-day Adventists,
Mormons, and Jehovah's Witnesses earlier in the nineteenth century. With minor variations, this premillennial apocalyptic theology is based on an absolute historical dualism that foresees a
catastrophic conflict between good and evil forces at the end of
history, after which the millennium of Christ's reign on earth will
be established. This means that all hopes for creating peace and
justice on a universal scale prior to this final apocalyptic conflict
are not only illusory but heretical. The Christian hope for premil-
lennialists is the "rapture" (1 Thess. 4:17), where it is believed all
true believers will be taken immediately to heaven before this final
conflict at Armageddon. From the perspective of other Christians,

however, the hope for the rapture in this form is an ignominious escape clause in the theology of those who are willing to prepare this final catastrophe for others while hoping to escape its suffering themselves. It is a "civil defense plan for the elect."

When the twentieth-century realities of the reestablishment of Israel and the seeding of our world with 50,000 nuclear weapons are added to this premillennial apocalyptic theology, we have the rudiments for Hal Lindsey's book, *The Late Great Planet Earth,* which has gone through fifty-nine printings and sold twenty million copies, making it the best-selling book in the United States in the twentieth century. Jerry Falwell used this theology to support the political program of preparation for nuclear war with Russia. In an interview published on March 4, 1981, in the *Los Angeles Times,* he predicted a nuclear war over Israel, in which "Russia will be the offender and will be ultimately totally destroyed," and went on to link it with the Christian hope for the completion of history: "We believe we're living in those days just prior to the Lord's coming."

Of far greater political import is the evidence that Ronald Reagan himself might have been influenced by this theology in making some of his policy decisions. In the same interview in the *Los Angeles Times,* Jerry Falwell quotes the President as having said to him in a private conversation, "Jerry, I sometimes believe we're heading very fast for Armageddon right now." And in a telephone conversation with Thomas Dine, executive director of the American-Israel Public Affairs Committee on October 18, 1983, President Reagan is reported to have said:

> You know, I turn back to your ancient prophets in the Old Testament and the signs foretelling Armageddon, and I find myself wondering if—if we're the generation that's going to see that come about. I don't know if you've noted any of those prophecies lately, but believe me, they certainly describe the times we're going through.[31]

Though these ideas come more from the book of Revelation in the New Testament than the Old Testament prophets to which the President referred, they are the very ideas of many of his evangelical Protestant supporters.

Fortunately, there is also evidence that President Reagan realized that these ideas are politically dangerous, if not absolutely so in the way that only theological ideas can be. When asked by journalists on the panel of his second debate with Walter Mondale on October 21, 1984, about the meaning of his earlier statements, the President replied, "No one knows whether those prophecies mean that Armageddon is a thousand years away or the day after tomorrow. So, I have never seriously warned and said we must plan according to Armageddon."[32] The *New York Times* editorialized following this debate:

> It is hard to believe that the President actually allows Armageddon theology to shape his policies toward the Soviet Union. Yet it was he who first portrayed the Russians as satanic and who keeps on talking about the final battle.[33]

The biblical basis for these political ideas is highly problematic in the light of a historical-critical understanding of the scripture. Professor Robert Jewett argues:

> Responsible interpretation requires us to understand biblical materials in the light of their unique historical circumstances rather than ruthlessly looting them for sentences and ideas that can be fitted into some modern apocalyptic outlook of New Testament writings, only one of which provides the key idea of a millennium, and none of which provides any real basis for dating the rapture. The exegetical method of the modern "doom boom" is essentially arbitrary, taking a few motifs from Revelation and Daniel, a couple of lines from Ezekiel and combining these with a single sentence from I Thessalonians and a half-dozen sentences from the Synoptic Gospels. When details like this are taken out of context and matched up jig-saw fashion with current events, the conclusion is that we are in the final generation and that there is nothing we can do to avert an atomic holocaust. This is an all-too-human conclusion, drastically at variance with most of the biblical writings themselves.[34]

My theological agreement with this biblical response to evangelical Protestantism's premillennial apocalypticism is evident from the biblical interpretation in the previous chapters. An adequate hermeneutic will rule out the absolute dualism of this apocalypticism while including some of its insights in a relative dualism that interprets the dialectics of our struggle for ultimate peace. The power of God to overcome our evil and create peace must be affirmed, not in the Davidic form of destructive force espoused by the Zealots that Jesus repudiated but in the living, liberating, reconciling form that Jesus embodied. The spiritual capacity of Christians to transcend the conflicts that divide our world can be affirmed and achieved, not in the form of an escapist "rapture" but in human spirits participating in the Holy Spirit, who enables the integrity of their self-integration through social relations so as to create personal peace in the struggle for reconciled communities and ultimately our nation-states.

With these theological perspectives, mainline Protestants can and must enter into genuine dialogue with evangelical Protestants about what Professor Jewett calls "Jesus' firm commitment to the prophetic idea that humans are responsible for history."[35] And the dialogue may move within a shared concern to place our political responsibility for history on as clear and responsible a christological foundation as possible. For we all must be aware in the light of our recent political history how momentous and even dangerous our theological ideas may be in so deeply divided a nuclear age.

Congregational Praxis and the Struggle for Peace

Churches in the United States who increasingly commit themselves to the praxis of universal peace must foster it by a praxis in congregations that are likely to be divided between their national and religious loyalties, as well as perhaps their racial, class, and even gender loyalties. The ecumenical conciliar process has affected approximately half of the American people enough that they have at least some attitude toward it. A recent Gallup poll of 1,522 in-person interviews found that 43 percent had no opinion about the National Council of Churches and 49 percent had none on the World Council of Churches. But of the slight majority who had an opinion, 50 percent believed the NCC to be "moderate," 26 percent thought it "liberal," and 24 percent felt it was "conservative." The attitude toward the WCC is similar, with 51 percent considering it moderate, 29 percent liberal, and 20 percent conservative.[36] These statistics suggest that participation in the ecumenical conciliar process is still nonexistent or in its beginning stages for too many congregations; they also indicate encouragingly that those who know some level of participation find it nonthreatening: that is, the majority who find it moderate may be sufficient to mediate the polarization of those who judge it liberal or conservative. It remains true, however, that self-described evangelicals in the poll were twice as likely to regard both councils as "liberal." So the more difficult task of mediation, as our analysis above has also made clear, remains in this group.

Given the relative size and growing activity of the Roman Catholic Church for peace and justice since Vatican Council II, it is also of great interest that Catholic respondents in this poll, though slightly less likely than Protestants to have an opinion, were more likely to see these Protestant and Orthodox councils as moderate. Only 20 percent of all Catholics, in contrast to 30 percent of all Protestants, regarded both councils as liberal. Our social analysis of U.S. churches above did not include the Roman Catholic Church, which has its own national conciliar process through the U.S. Catholic Conference and its universal conciliar process through the Vatican. It is of great significance, however, that a growing number of Catholic archdioceses across the nation are full members of statewide ecumenical agencies. A 1981 study revealed that 71 of 180 dioceses had joined the conciliar process at this more local level.[37] Thus an increasing number of judicatories and their congregations have an institutionalized conciliar process for consultation on missional concerns for peace and justice that also includes Roman Catholic colleagues. The data of the General Social Survey used above for Protestants also indicate that Roman Catholics, on the whole, describe themselves as less conservative than mainline or evangelical Protestants, and that 45 percent of them are identified with the Democratic party as compared to 20 percent with the Republican party.[38] Thus a conciliar process that includes Roman Catholics provides a significant balance to the traditional political preferences of Protestants.

This social analysis indicates that the christological understanding of universal peace articulated in this study may fruitfully interact with the context for praxis in U.S. churches. Though the threat of polarization to any significant consensus is great, this is to be expected when peace is understood as dialectical in a relatively dualistic history whose salvation is achieved only through the struggles for creative transformation. But the possibility for moving toward genuinely new consensus on peace and justice policies on national and international issues requires a praxis that is both courageous and compassionate in congregations that are genuinely open to a dialogical process.

There are both denominational and nondenominational peacemaking programs that are gathering significant experience in the guiding of such praxis. The Presbyterian Peacemaking Program is one that has done significant work at denominational and local levels in interaction with the ecumenical conciliar process. The heart of this program at the local level is to create a "holistic style of peacemaking ministry" in the congregations through their "worship, education, pastoral care, group life, governance, and outreach."[39] This means that in the worship life of the congregation week after week those whom some consider "enemies" are prayed for with specificity such as prayers for a bounteous Soviet harvest, and that the social and political as well as the personal dimensions clearly inherent in biblical texts on peace are interpreted in the sermons week by week.

It also means that pastoral care will deal skillfully with the deeply felt anxieties that the nuclear era and the arms race have spawned in many persons in every congregation. Many have suffered nuclear nightmares with little opportunity or guidance as to how to resolve suppressed anxiety in their spiritual lives. Some feel a constant need to increase their sense of security without knowing how. The more they have supported the national-security state, the less secure they have felt. They have had to numb themselves to the terrifying consequences of the nuclear arms race and pretend they believe in the protection provided by nuclear deterrence.[40] Such unresolved anxiety can lead to the schizoid tendencies that R. D. Laing has analyzed in his psychiatric study of *The Divided Self.*[41] Using Laing's work, Ira Chernus suggests that such "masked selves" can create a nexus of what we have called external relations "whose apparent reality is so compelling that the very existence of the true self is virtually forgotten . . . a societal fantasy world which is mistaken for the only possible world in which human beings might live."[42] The danger is that the "firm resolve" to deter the enemy created in a schizoid nexus may reflect schizoid fears not only of nuclear annihilation but of all flexibility and change that may alone move toward genuine security, though at first it may increase feelings of insecurity.

Pastoral care must provide a new possibility for authentic internal relations in a context of genuine acceptance where members of Christian congregations have the opportunity to tell and hear what it means for them to live in a nuclear age. Richard Watts reports three benefits from such sharing:

> First, telling pent-up, unexpressed stories is therapeutic in and of itself. Second, people tend to listen respectfully, sensitively, to one another's stories; that respect then carries over to the church's wrestling with controversial questions of how to be involved with such issues. Third, people who are enabled to express their own feelings and experiences are afterwards far more receptive than before to new learnings.[43]

Given the depth of the alienated divisions in our world, such pastoral care will not expect easily to resolve all conflicting commitments of various members of the congregation. This is especially true for those whose religion has provided them a "crusade" rationale for their commitments to national security. Herbert York, the first director of the Lawrence Livermore Laboratory, the leading defense research facility in our country, wrote in his *Race to Oblivion:*

> The majority of the key individual promoters of the arms race derive a very large part of their self-esteem from their participation in what they believe to be an essential—even a holy—cause.[44]

Those Christians who understand their commitments to nuclear forms of national defense to be a "holy cause" will have to be dealt with dialogically over a long period, so that they at least consider the alternative understandings of peace articulated in our discussion as one example of what is emerging through the ecumenical conciliar process.

This means that peacemaking shall have to include many and continuing forms of Christian education within the church school and the various groups of the church, ranging from biblical and theological studies of *shalom* to domestic and international violence. Richard Watts's insight at this point is also helpful:

Some persons who are simply unable to cope with issues of nuclear weapons may be very ready to become part of a group studying how to handle conflict in the family. As they discover that a "win-win" style is more fruitful than a "win-lose" approach to conflict at home, they may be encouraged to imagine what a "win-win" style might do for arms negotiations in Geneva.[45]

The aim of the congregational praxis of peace should be creative personal and interpersonal transformation that will also empower the struggle for social transformation toward peace. Some members will be led to organize ecumenically to work on such issues as poverty and homelessness, spouse and child abuse, foreign policies and disarmament. A holistic style of congregational peacemaking should provide a new legitimacy for those members of the congregation who understand their attempts at systemic change to be a radical form of Christian witness. They should be seen as part of a congregational continuum that encourages all of its members to personally authentic forms of public witness.

Such a panorama means that congregations will have to know a sufficient grace in their sacramental interaction that they can allow controversy and conflicting stances to emerge and engage each other. Administrative and governance structures in the congregations will have to learn techniques of conflict management that enhance an open negotiation toward genuine consensus, as well as practice the gracious patience and forgiveness that alone finally sustains Christian life together in an alienated world. There may well be some members who, for long stretches, shall have to agree to disagree while remaining open to the authentic concerns and analyses of the others, thus remaining open to the possibility of creative transformation through genuinely internal relations.

Spiritually, this means that all our congregations will have to find their own ways to combine the inward and outward journeys that authentic peace praxis requires. True community on the basis of deep internal relations grounded sacramentally in God must be created. Careful critical reflection upon social and political reality in the light of a Christology of peace must be fostered. Participation in ecumenical efforts for social change must be encouraged and legitimated.[46] When the praxis of peace becomes so comprehensive a spirituality, then the ecumenical conciliar vision expressed in such programs as "Peacemaking: The Believers' Calling" may be concretely realized through our congregations:

> How will peace be achieved? By disarmament? Certainly, but not only by disarmament. By global economic reform? Certainly, but not only by global economic reform. By the change of political structures? Certainly, but not only by the change of political structures. Basically, at the heart, it is a matter of the way we see the world through the eyes of Christ. It is a matter of praying and yearning. It is an inner response to God, who loves the whole world and whose Spirit calls for and empowers the making of peace.[47]

Public Policy Reformulation in the Praxis of Peace

The Christian's inner response to God, if it is a genuine sacramental participation in God's trinitarian relationality, will inevitably be joined with a total response to the world God is creating and redeeming. This means that such concerns as disarmament and national and global justice will be an organic and necessary part of our total spirituality. But such a comprehensive personal spirituality, according to the Christology of peace we have been articulating, must be organically linked with a comprehensive ecclesial participation that in turn comprehends itself as a sacrament of the unity of humankind. With such an understanding it is impossible to be satisfied with the peace witness of only a prophetic minority within the church, who may witness through dramatic action to an alternative life-style. As grateful as one must be for the stimulus to the church of such heroic witness, the Christian praxis of peace must seek public policy reformulation through dialogical consensus in the whole church as it seeks to influence its whole society.

Churches must thus learn to act effectively in both their national context and the transnational context of the ecumenical church. This means following a coalition strategy that seeks maximum support for realistic changes at particular points in time. As difficult as it may be in so dangerous an age of continuing nuclear confrontation, the churches must accept a strategy that recognizes peace as a process that cannot be accomplished all at once.

What can be authentically accomplished through an open political process requires coalition with significant elements of the political center. This obviously does not mean that the church will allow its Christology of peace to be decided by majority vote, but it does require critical cooperation with those leaders of the political center who are in the church or willing to be in dialogue with the church. Leaders of the Dutch Inter-Church Peace Council, who have been successful in leading a majority of the Dutch population to support the unilateral removal of all nuclear weapons from the Netherlands, agree with W. A. Williams that real changes in democracies depend "on the extent to which calm and confident conservatives can see and bring themselves to act upon the validity of a radical analysis."[48] Political decisions on public policy reformulation cannot be made "over the heads" of church members or citizens; they must be given opportunity to engage in the dialogue that leads to the negotiation of such policy changes.

The experience of the leading Protestant and Roman Catholic churches in the Netherlands is suggestive for other churches. Before the Netherlands Reformed Church adopted its "Pastoral Letter on Atomic Weapons" in 1980, it sent a preliminary draft to its 1,500 congregations in 1979 and received more than 700 written responses, which were taken into account in the final drafting. Before the Dutch Roman Catholic bishops published their "Pastoral Letter on Peace and Justice" in 1983, they sponsored a "discussion round" in their parishes in which 40,000 persons participated, and they received more than 2,200 written reactions.[49] This is the kind of open process that is necessary if the churches' witness on disarmament is to be authentically supported by large proportions of its membership and have a strong effect in its society.

To gain the support of elements of the political center, the churches may not engage in the kind of power politics that seeks to change international balances of power. The same Dutch polls that showed a majority supporting the churches' position on unilateral denuclearization of the Netherlands also showed strong support for continuing membership in NATO and the need to maintain military equilibrium between East and West.[50] This means that, except in situations of dire distress, the church normally must seek to transform the existing power structures toward peace, following a coalition strategy in an open political process. Reflecting on the experience of the European churches, I came to a conclusion then that still seems valid now:

> Thus a church peace strategy in any of our societies, if it is to gain sufficient domestic support, must neither aim, nor be interpretable as aiming, at destabilization of existing balances of power between East and West. It is a moot question, but I think that it may never be appropriate for the church as such to function in *realpolitik* in so direct a way. The moral dimensions of the church's peace strategy are fatally obscured when churches allow themselves to be drawn so completely into power politics.[51]

Such political wisdom at the national level must be matched by openness to new learning and new possibilities at the transnational ecumenical level. There are Americans who have interpreted European peace movements as "neutralism or pacifism." A. J. Sligty, spokesman for the Netherlands Ministry of Defense, replied, "Those Americans who use those words confuse [neutrality] with the real concern that people who live in this part of the world feel. . . . It is the concern of people who are living on the battlefield."[52] There are approximately 6,000 nuclear warheads aimed at the Warsaw Pact nations deployed in Western Europe alone, matched by Soviet missiles aimed at the West. None of them requires more than five minutes to reach their targets, requiring a hair-trigger launch-on-warning posture if they are not to be wiped out in a first-strike attack. A "battlefield" defined by Hiroshima plus Nagasaki multiplied by 6,000 on hair-trigger alert may well give many Europeans a sensitivity to the threat of nuclear war that North Americans don't yet feel so immediately. Much might be learned from them about both their and our danger through the dialogues of the ecumenical church.

Such ecumenical learning must come through dialogues with both East and West. The churches of the (East) German Democratic Republic (GDR) have developed reasoned positions on the politics of peace from which North American Christians might also benefit. They have studied carefully the deliberation of the Palme Commission and have come to support national and international policies that replace the failed policy of mutual deterrence with the Palme Commission's principle of "common security."[53] The Synod of the Federation of Protestant Churches in the GDR, meeting in Halle in 1982, went beyond their earlier "rejection of the spirit of the system of deterrence" to support clear positions on the disarmament debates in their own society:

> The rejection of the spirit of the system of deterrence should become effective not only in verbal explanations and exemplary action, but also in political plans through concretely discriminating judgments. Such judgments must submit themselves to political argumentation.[54]

Churches whose representatives have entered into such ecumenical dialogue have achieved consensus on principles that should guide all churches striving for Christ's universal peace. The Sixth Assembly of the World Council of Churches, meeting in Vancouver, B.C., in 1983, appealed to all of its member churches to:

> Challenge military and militaristic policies that lead to disastrous distortions of foreign policy
> Counter the trend to characterize those of other nations and ideologies as the "enemy" through the promotion of hatred and prejudice
> Assist in demythologizing current doctrines of national security and elaborate new concepts of security based on justice and the rights of people[55]

What is now necessary to fulfill the praxis of the Christology of peace articulated here is to move the ecumenical dialogue that leads to such conclusions into the local judicatories and congregations, who feel alienated from the positions of their ecclesial elite when their thinking on such issues is left largely to the guidance of the security ideologies of their governments interpreted through their mass media.

The ecumenical churches as sacramental communities of the work of the universal Holy Spirit are what is crucial here. The East German churches did not just reject nuclear deterrence, they rejected "the *spirit* of the system of deterrence"; in other words, the integration of personal and communal energies that is grounded in anxiety and focused on military deterrence is an evil, destructive, demonic spirit. When human spirits are redemptively integrated by the Holy Spirit, they can be grounded in faith and hope and be focused on the common security of peace. The Christian World Conference on "Life and Peace," held in Uppsala, Sweden, in 1983, celebrated and articulated this spiritual reality:

> We, who come from various different churches, see a great sign of hope in the efforts toward the unity of Christendom. Precisely at this point in history, where divisions threaten the mere survival of humanity, the Holy Spirit moves his people to discover and publicly acknowledge this unity.[56]

North American churches are increasingly articulating the implications of this new spirit, the most celebrated recent instances being the Roman Catholic bishops' pastoral letter on "The Challenge of Peace" in May 1983 and the United Methodist bishops' pastoral letter "In Defense of Creation" in April 1986. Both pastoral letters morally condemn nuclear warfare as murder and conclude, counter to current U.S. and NATO policy, that no use, and thus certainly no "first use," of nuclear weapons may be justified. Both advocate a nuclear freeze and oppose the development of the MX and Trident II missiles and the Strategic Defense Initiative. Their only real difference is that the United Methodist bishops went further in saying an unconditional no not only to the use of nuclear weapons but to their long-term possession for deterrence, while their Roman Catholic colleagues only placed "strict moral conditions" on the continual possession of nuclear weapons for the sake of deterrence. At this point, they reflect the difference in the current ecumenical consensus of their confreres in the World Council of Churches for the United Methodists and the Vatican for the Roman Catholics.

These recent pastoral letters were the result of long processes of consultation. The Roman Catholic Bishops' Committee considered 700 pages of commentary received in response to their first draft and an additional 500 pages after their second draft. They also consulted with representatives of the U.S. government between the second and third drafts.[57] The United Methodist bishops began with two days of testimony in Washington, D.C., in July 1985 from political, military, scientific, theological, and ethical representatives. Consultation in each Bishops Area generated extensive response to the first draft, which was considered in two further meetings of the drafting committee before the Pastoral Letter was unanimously adopted by the Council of Bishops.[58] This kind of open consultative praxis is exactly what is required from the standpoint of a Christology of peace.

It must be emphasized again, however, that such open consultation must especially include the concerns of the marginalized and oppressed. That is, the concerns for peace as reconciliation must be dialectically related to peace as justice. Some black, feminist, and third world Christians resist a focus on disarmament and East-West reconciliation because they fear it will obscure their concern for crucial justice issues. This means that the praxis of peace must remain utterly realistic about the depth and extent of conflict in our world, whether the cultural conflict of feminists in a patriarchal society, the economic conflict of liberationist movements in neocolonialist societies, or the political conflict of black peoples in racist societies.

There will likewise be no authentic East-West reconciliation until the human rights issues in the Soviet Union and Eastern Europe and the United States and Western Europe are adequately addressed and redressed, just as there will be no peace in Southern Africa as long as apartheid is practiced in South Africa and Namibia; no peace in the Middle East until Israel has secure, internationally recognized borders and the Palestinians receive their human rights in Israel and their own secure state; no peace in Central America until the exploitation of the poor by national elites allied with multinational corporations stops.

These multiple justice issues are too complex to be analyzed here. We can note, however, that the ecumenical churches have significantly addressed these issues. We have already reviewed in chapter 5 how the World Council of Churches' Programme to Combat Racism has withstood the internal controversies it has engendered and provided the churches a significant means for supporting black liberation around the world. Ecumenical processes of consultation have also begun to articulate the churches' belief in the holistic character of human rights as expressing the relational reality of the whole human community. Such discussion has led to a virtual consensus on the complementarity of the liberal tradition of civil and political rights and the socialist tradition of economic, social, and cultural rights:

Those human rights first formulated in the liberal tradition, which seek to protect the essential dignity of each person from violation by the power of the state or any other corporate structure (such as the churches in the eighteenth century and the economic corporations of the twentieth century), are grounded in the universal relation to the true God who transcends all such potentially idolatrous national and corporate structures. . . . Human rights first formulated in the socialist tradition, which seek to create and protect justice in organic industrial communities, must be added to the liberal tradition so that human dignity under God may be realized concretely in historical societies. Only through adequate and just social structures may basic human needs be universally met, and thus fundamental human rights be realized. But, likewise, only in human and participatory structures, kept constitutionally open to the many-faceted human critique which protects them from becoming idolatrous, may the personal freedom created and guaranteed by our God-relation be realized and protected as a fundamental human right.[59]

The ecumenical process that has led toward such consensus is reflected in the special issue of *Soundings* on "The East-West Encounter Over Human Rights: Its Religious and Social Context," with contributions from scholars in Hungary, Poland, the Soviet Union, and the United States.[60] The essay quoted in the paragraph above began as a study project of the Faith and Order Commission of the National Council of Churches and reflects international study processes of Lutheran, Reformed, and Roman Catholic churches. It remains, of course, unfortunately true that this emergent consensus on the ecumenical level has not yet sufficiently penetrated the preaching, teaching, and dialogue of most congregations to have a chance of really emerging there. Thus the concerns for freedom and the concerns for social justice often remain ideologically highly polarized in too many Christian communities.

There is reason to hope, however, in what has already been accomplished through the ecumenical conciliar process, that the peace praxis of the churches may continue to mature as the Holy Spirit enables participation in the loving relationality of the trinitarian God revealed in the life, teaching, death, and resurrection of Jesus. We may and must learn a praxis that combines peace and justice, liberation and reconciliation, personal freedom and social equality in the reign of God where Christ's blessing allows "peacemakers" authentically to become "the children of God."

Notes

Chapter 1: The Universality of God and the Particularity of Peace

1. Augustine, *The City of God,* XIX.12.

2. Pinchas Lapide and Jürgen Moltmann, *Jewish Monotheism and Christian Trinitarian Doctrine,* tr. Leonard Swidler (Philadelphia: Fortress Press, 1981), p. 91. Cf. the comprehensive research and the irenic conclusions of Robert Jewett, "The Law and Coexistence of Jesus and Gentiles in Romans," *Interpretation,* vol. 39, no. 4 (Oct. 1985), pp. 341–356.

3. Cf. H. Richard Niebuhr, *The Social Sources of Denominationalism* (New York: Henry Holt & Co., 1929; New York: Meridian Books, 1957).

4. Cf. my earlier essay on "The Place of Ideology in Theology," *Journal of Ecumenical Studies,* vol. 15, no. 1 (Winter 1978), pp. 41–53.

5. Wolfhart Pannenberg, *Jesus—God and Man* (Philadelphia: Westminster Press, 1968), pp. 47–48.

6. Gibson Winter, *Scientific and Ethical Perspectives on Social Process* (New York: Macmillan Co., 1966), p. 54.

7. The work of Erik H. Erikson is especially instructive here; see especially *Identity and the Life Cycle* (New York: W. W. Norton & Co., 1959, 1980).

8. For an insightful and provocative interpretation of this theme in relation to contemporary experience, I know nothing better than Prof. James A. Sander's lecture, "The New History: Joseph Our Brother," interpreting Genesis 37:1–11 and Matthew 5:43–48, delivered to and published by the Ministers and Missionaries Benefit Board, American Baptist Convention, 1968.

9. This certainly was my experience in studying theology when neo-

orthodox interpretations were dominant, especially with Reinhold Niebuhr. For insight into the Wisdom/blessing motif that is equally intrinsic to scripture, cf. Claus Westermann, *What Does the Old Testament Say About God?* (Atlanta: John Knox Press, 1979), and Walter Brueggemann, *In Man We Trust: The Neglected Side of Biblical Faith* (Richmond: John Knox Press, 1972).

10. Frederick Herzog, *God-Walk* (Maryknoll, N.Y.: Orbis Books, 1988), p. xii.

11. Cf. Rosemary Radford Ruether, *Faith and Fratricide* (New York: Seabury Press, 1974).

12. For this notion of an "enhypostatic union," see D. M. Baillie, *God Was in Christ* (New York: Charles Scribner's Sons, 1948), pp. 85–93.

Chapter 2: The Jewishness of Jesus and the Struggle for Peace

1. Elie Wiesel, in *Jerusalem, Most Fair of Cities* (France, 1981), p. 11.

2. Cf. David Flusser, *Jesus,* tr. R. Walls (New York: Herder & Herder, 1969). Professor Flusser has even written, "I do not think many Jews would object if the messiah when he comes again was the Jew Jesus," in *Concilium,* new series, 5.10 (1974), p. 71.

3. Pinchas Lapide and Jürgen Moltmann, *Jewish Monotheism and Christian Trinitarian Doctrine,* tr. Leonard Swidler (Philadelphia: Fortress Press, 1981), p. 83.

4. Robert Jewett has written of this development: "After the first of these disastrous expressions of zealous crusading, Judaism turned away from this legacy under the leadership of the Jamnian rabbis, creating a non-nationalistic form of the Jewish faith. The long term consequence was that Israel was in fact 'saved.' A remnant faithful to the Torah was preserved from zealotism, chauvinism, militarism, and violent apocalypticism. . . . By abandoning zealous violence as a means of bringing the messianic age, Rabbinic Judaism was able to preserve the vision of international peace as part of a messianic future," in "The Law and Coexistence of Jews and Gentiles in Romans," *Interpretation,* vol. 39, no. 4 (Oct. 1985), p. 355.

5. Allen Verhey has put this point very well in his study of the ethics of the New Testament: *The Great Reversal* (Grand Rapids: Wm. B. Eerdmans Publishing Co., 1984), p. 15: "It becomes crucially important, then, that Jesus describes that action of God differently than apocalyptic literature typically did. He revises the material content of apocalyptic expectation. He still expects the reign of God to bring judgment and salvation, liberation and security. He still expects 'a great reversal' of this present

age. But the nationalistic hope for Israel's lordship over and revenge against the nation is strikingly absent (e.g., Lk. 4:16ff.)."

6. Edward Schillebeeckx, *Jesus: An Experiment in Christology,* tr. Hubert Hoskins (New York: Seabury Press, 1979), p. 32. I am glad to acknowledge that much of what follows in this chapter depends on Schillebeeckx's monumental scholarship, which, as Robert Jewett judges, is "surely the most elaborate effort in modern times to incorporate the insights of biblical scholarship into a christological project," in "New Testament Christology: The Current Dialogue Between Systematic Theologians and New Testament Scholars," *Semeia. Christology and Exegesis: New Approaches,* vol. 30 (1985), p. 5.

7. Philo, *Quaest. in Exodum* II.29.

8. This history is recounted in Josephus, *The Jewish Wars* 6:212–213.

9. Richard A. Horsley, *Jesus and the Spiral of Violence* (San Francisco: Harper & Row, 1987), especially pp. x–xi, 56–57. Horsley's social-historical thesis that Jesus was closer to the nonviolent struggles of some of his Jewish compatriots also fits my basic theological perspective; that is, I affirm more continuity between Jesus' gospel of peace and Judaism than European advocates of the Zealot hypothesis affirm, and I see the social struggle for justice as a dimension of the Christian gospel of peace illumined by liberation theologies.

10. Most important in this regard has been the declaration of the Roman Catholic Church in Vatican Council II, "Declaration on the Relationship of the Church to Non-Christian Religions" *(Nostra aetate).*

11. Here the work of Christian groups like the Palestine Human Rights Campaign differs little from some fully Jewish, and even Zionist, religious groups like Oz ve Shalom.

Chapter 3: The Crucifixion of Jesus and the Dialectic of Peace

1. Paul Ricoeur, "El conflicto: signo de contradicción y de unidad?" *Criterio* (Buenos Aires), no. 1668 (May 24, 1973), pp. 253–254.

2. Jürgen Moltmann, *The Crucified God,* tr. R. A. Wilson and John Bowden (London: SCM Press, 1974), p. 1. Professor Lapide, as an Orthodox Jew, shares much of Moltmann's perspective after Auschwitz and thus can enter deeply into this dialectic and dialogue with him. See *Jewish Monotheism and Christian Trinitarian Doctrine,* tr. Leonard Swidler (Philadelphia: Fortress Press, 1981), pp. 61 and 66.

3. Cf. Alfred North Whitehead, *Process and Reality,* corr. ed., ed. David Roy Griffin and Donald W. Sherburne (New York: Free Press, 1978), pp. 342–343, and Bernard Loomer, "Two Conceptions of Power," *Process Studies* 6:1.

4. John Wesley, *Wesley's Standard Sermons,* ed. Edw. H. Sugden (London: Epworth Press, 1921), vol. 2, pp. 224–225.

5. Paul Tillich, "Das Dämonische, ein Beitrag zur Sinndeutung der Geschichte," in *The Interpretation of History,* tr. N. A. Rasetzki and Elsa L. Talmey (New York: Charles Scribner's Sons, 1936), pp. 77–122. Cf. Ronald Stone, *Paul Tillich's Radical Social Thought* (Atlanta: John Knox Press, 1980), pp. 58–61.

6. Timothy Smith, "Holiness and Radicalism in Nineteenth-Century America," in Theodore Runyon, ed., *Sanctification and Liberation* (Nashville: Abingdon Press, 1981), pp. 137–138.

7. John Wesley published thirteen royalist tracts and open letters opposing the "anarchistic" American rebels. Francis Asbury wrote of him that "there is not a man in the world so obnoxious to the American politicians as our dear old Daddy."

8. Rupert E. Davies, "Justification, Sanctification, and the Liberation of the Person," in Runyon, ed., *Sanctification and Liberation,* p. 80, emphasis added.

9. Richard M. Nixon, quoted in Robert Bellah, "American Civil Religion in the 1970's," in Russell E. Richey and Donald G. Jones, eds., *American Civil Religion* (New York: Harper & Row, 1974), pp. 259–260.

10. John Kent, "Methodism and Social Change in Britain," in Runyon, ed., *Sanctification and Liberation,* pp. 89 and 97.

11. Moltmann, *The Crucified God,* p. 245.

12. Ibid., pp. 246–247.

13. Ibid., p. 277, emphasis added.

14. Ibid., p. 249.

15. Ibid., p. 3.

16. This remains true even though Mark perhaps exaggerated the disciples' misunderstanding and defection to fit his theology of the "messianic secret."

17. Edward Schillebeeckx, *Jesus: An Experiment in Christology,* tr. Hubert Hoskins (New York: Seabury Press, 1979), p. 306.

Chapter 4: The Resurrection of Christ and the Spirit of Peace

1. Professor Pinchas Lapide, an Orthodox Jew, eloquently makes this point in a way that is astonishing to most Christians, and not only the German congregation he was addressing: "If he [Jesus] had shown himself as the resurrected One, not only to the 530 Jewish witnesses but to the entire population, all Jews would have become followers of Jesus. To me this would have had only one imaginable consequence: the church, baptism, the forgiveness of sins, the cross, everything today which is Christian

would have remained an inner-Jewish institution, and you, my dear friend, would today still be offering horsemeat to Wotan on the Godesberg. Put in other words, I see in the fact that the Easter experience was imparted to only some Jews the finger of God indicating that . . . the time was ripe that the faith in One God should be carried into the world of the Gentiles."

This, of course, would not be so astounding if all Christians understood Paul in Romans 9–11 as well as Professor Lapide does. See Lapide and Moltmann, *Jewish Monotheism and Christian Trinitarian Doctrine*, tr. Leonard Swidler (Philadelphia: Fortress Press, 1981), pp. 68–69.

2. Edward Schillebeeckx, *Christ: The Experience of Jesus as Lord*, tr. John Bowden (New York: Seabury Press, 1980), p. 794.

3. Paul Tillich, *Systematic Theology* (Chicago: University of Chicago Press, 1963), vol. 3, pp. 27–28.

4. Ibid., p. 111.

5. Ibid., p. 112.

6. For a more complete discussion than is possible here, see Schillebeeckx, *Christ: The Experience of Jesus as Lord*, pp. 427–432.

7. Martin Buber, *I and Thou*, tr. Walter Kaufmann (New York: Charles Scribner's Sons, 1970), p. 99.

8. Friedrich Nietzsche, "Der tolle Mensch," in *Die fröliche Wissenschaft*, no. 125, quoted by Jürgen Moltmann, *The Trinity and the Kingdom*, tr. Margaret Kohl (San Francisco: Harper & Row, 1981), p. 13.

9. Rudolf Bultmann, "What Does It Mean to Speak of God?" in *Faith and Understanding* (London: SCM Press, 1969), p. 63.

10. Karl Barth, *Church Dogmatics*, I/1, p. 349.

11. Karl Barth, *Church Dogmatics*, II/2, p. 166.

12. Tillich, *Systematic Theology*, vol. 3, p. 224.

13. Moltmann, *The Trinity and the Kingdom*, p. 4.

14. Ibid., p. 197.

15. Augustine, *On the Trinity*, VIII. 10. Cf. Cyril C. Richardson, "The Enigma of the Trinity," *A Companion to the Study of St. Augustine*, ed. Roy W. Battenhouse (New York: Oxford University Press, 1955), esp. pp. 246–248.

16. For a brief discussion of the contributions of Basil, Gregory of Nyssa, and Gregory of Nazianzus, see J. N. D. Kelly, *Early Christian Doctrines*, 2nd ed. (New York: Harper & Brothers., 1960), pp. 258–269, esp. pp. 264–267. Cf. his *The Athanasian Creed* (New York: Harper & Row, 1964), pp. 73–86.

17. Although this concept has been widely ignored in Western thought, the modern philosopher of science and metaphysician Alfred North Whitehead thought this doctrine "of mutual immanence in the divine nature" to be the only "fundamental metaphysical doctrine to have im-

proved upon Plato." See his *Adventures of Ideas* (New York: Free Press, 1933, 1961), pp. 167–168.

18. M. L. Brownsberger, "From the Other Side of the Pulpit," *The Christian Century*, vol. 103, no. 25 (Aug. 27–Sept. 3, 1986), p. 747.

19. Ibid., p. 748.

20. Ibid.

21. Moltmann, *The Trinity and the Kingdom*, p. 199.

22. Ibid.

23. Ibid.

Chapter 5: The Unity of Christ, Community of Trinity, and Universality of Peace

1. Fydor Dostoevski, *Correspondence* I (Paris: Cälmänn-Levy, 1961), p. 157, quoted by Leonardo Boff, *Jesus Christ Liberator*, tr. Patrick Hughes (Maryknoll, N.Y.: Orbis Books, 1978), p. 99.

2. Edward Schillebeeckx, *Christ: The Experience of Jesus as Lord*, tr. John Bowden (New York: Seabury Press, 1980), p. 430.

3. Cf. Wolfhart Pannenberg, *Jesus—God and Man*, tr. Lewis Wilkins and Duane Priebe (Philadelphia: Westminster Press, 1968), pp. 160–161.

4. See Matt. 11:16–19; 23:34–39 and parallels in Luke. Cf. Walter Kasper, *Jesus the Christ*, tr. V. Green (New York: Paulist Press, 1976), pp. 186–187.

5. Schillebeeckx, *Christ: The Experience of Jesus as Lord*, p. 196. My agreement as to the importance of Ephesians for the churches' witness to peace may be seen in my two earlier works: *Must Walls Divide?* (New York: Friendship Press, 1981), esp. pp. 32 and 88, and *The Moral Rejection of Nuclear Deterrence* (New York: Friendship Press, 1985), esp. p. 2.

6. "The Definition of Chalcedon," *Documents of the Christian Church*, ed. H. Bettenson (New York: Oxford University Press, 1947), p. 73.

7. St. Gregory Nazianzus, Epist. 101, quoted in Leonardo Boff, *Jesus Christ Liberator*, p. 186.

8. John B. Cobb, Jr., *Christ in a Pluralistic Age* (Philadelphia: Westminster Press, 1975), p. 166.

9. Pannenberg, *Jesus—God and Man*, p. 166.

10. Ibid., p. 165.

11. Cobb, *Christ in a Pluralistic Age*, pp. 167–169.

12. Alfred North Whitehead, *Adventures of Ideas* (New York: Free Press, 1933, 1961), p. 167.

13. Ibid., pp. 168–169.

14. Cobb, *Christ in a Pluralistic Age*, p. 59.

15. Ibid., pp. 69–70.

16. Whitehead's metaphysics was formulated in three volumes written in the early years of his professorship in the Harvard University philosophy department after a long career in Cambridge and London as a mathematician and philosopher of science: *Science and the Modern World* (New York: Macmillan Co., 1925); *Religion in the Making* (New York: Macmillan Co., 1926); and *Process and Reality* (New York: Macmillan Co., 1929). See especially the corrected edition (1978) of the last, his magnum opus, esp. pp. 244–245.

17. Alfred North Whitehead, *Process and Reality*, corr. ed., ed. David Ray Griffin and Donald W. Sherburne (New York: Free Press, 1978), p. 244.

18. Cobb, *Christ in a Pluralistic Age*, p. 72.

19. Ibid., p. 75.

20. Ibid., p. 77.

21. Ibid., p. 140.

22. The fact that Cobb knew Moltmann only through his *Theology of Hope* when he was writing this book, though the English translation of Moltmann's *The Crucified God* appeared in 1974, perhaps partly explains Cobb's failure to discuss the crucifixion. But even in Cobb's later *Process Theology as Political Theology* (Philadelphia: Westminster Press, 1982), where he more explicitly deals with Moltmann's later work, Cobb fails to deal at length with Moltmann's understanding of the crucifixion.

23. Cobb, *Christ in a Pluralistic Age*, p. 75.

24. Jürgen Moltmann, *The Crucified God*, tr. R. A. Wilson and John Bowden (London: SCM Press, 1974), pp. 242–243.

25. Ibid., p. 245.

26. Cf. the discussion in the last section of chapter 3.

27. I find my understanding here akin to that of Walter Kasper in his *Jesus the Christ*, p. 187: "The theme of the wisdom of God as the folly of the cross, resisted and contradicted by the wisdom of this world, is found again in 1 Cor. 1 and 2. Even the theology of the cross therefore cannot be played off against a sapiental Christology within a universal horizon: but it is an important corrective, so that God's wisdom in Jesus Christ and the wisdom of the world are not confused and the cross of Christ is not 'made void' (1 Cor. 1:17)."

28. Moltmann, *The Crucified God*, pp. 247–249.

29. Cobb, *Christ in a Pluralistic Age*, p. 155.

30. Ibid., p. 257.

31. Ibid., p. 260.

32. Ibid., p. 261.

33. Ibid., p. 262. Cf. Whitehead, *Process and Reality*, corr. ed. 1978, pp. 342–351.

34. Cobb, *Christ in a Pluralistic Age,* p. 264.

35. Cobb, *Process Theology as Political Theology,* p. 72.

36. Ibid., quoted from Schubert Ogden, *Faith and Freedom: Towards a Theology of Liberation* (Nashville: Abingdon Press, 1979), p. 34.

37. Cobb, *Process Theology as Political Theology,* pp. 73–75 and 78–81.

38. Ibid., p. 80.

39. Schubert Ogden, *The Point of Christology* (San Francisco: Harper & Row, 1982). For his clear response to liberationist concerns see especially pp. 91–95.

40. Ibid., pp. 120 and 122.

41. Ibid., pp. 124–125.

42. Ibid., p. 131, emphasis added.

43. Ibid., p. 144.

44. Ibid., p. 145; emphasis is in the text.

45. Ibid., p. 163; emphasis is in the text.

46. Leonardo Boff, *Liberating Grace,* tr. John Drury (Maryknoll, N.Y.: Orbis Books, 1979), p. 203.

47. Ibid., p. 211.

48. Leonardo Boff, *Jesus Christ Liberator,* tr. Patrick Hughes (Maryknoll, N.Y.: Orbis Books, 1978), esp. pp. 253–254 and 258–261.

49. Ibid., p. 269.

50. Ibid., p. 287, emphasis added.

51. Ibid., p. 289.

52. Ibid., p. 291.

53. Susan Brooks Thistlethwaite, *Metaphors for the Contemporary Church* (New York: Pilgrim Press, 1983), pp. 114–115.

54. Barbara Rogers, *Race: No Peace Without Justice,* Appendix (Geneva: World Council of Churches, 1980), p. 119.

55. Ibid., p. 120 and p. 3.

56. Ibid., pp. 3–5.

57. Ibid., pp. 6–7.

58. Leonardo Boff, *Church: Charism and Power,* tr. John W. Diercksmeier (New York: Crossroad Publishing Co., 1986).

59. Ibid., pp. 159–160.

60. Ibid., p. 164.

61. David Tracy, *Plurality and Ambiguity* (San Francisco: Harper & Row, 1987), p. 13. He illustrates this in terms of contemporary interpretations of Luke-Acts, which is so important for our interpretation of Christ as the incarnation of that "creative transformation" leading toward peace; "Luke-Acts is still received in conflicting ways by very different Christian groups: charismatics appealing to the role of the Spirit in these texts,

liberation and political theologies insisting upon the preferential option for the poor, liberal Christians content with Luke's rather commonsensical account of Jesus, Barthians anxious to show how Luke resembles a nineteenth-century realistic novel rendering the true identity of the main character through its history like narrative" (pp. 13–14). The hermeneutic we have used in developing this Christology of peace has tried to integrate the charismatic, liberation-political, and Barthian modes of interpretation, while recognizing that much remains ambiguous.

62. Ibid., p. 111.

63. *Peacemaking Without Division* is the title of an excellent guide for congregational workshops on peace witness and action developed by Patricia Washburn and Robert Gribbon (Washington, D.C., The Alban Institute, 1986).

64. Cited ibid., p. 31.

65. Tracy, *Plurality and Ambiguity,* p. 114.

Chapter 6: The Universal Church and the Praxis of Peace

1. "The Epistle to Diognetus," V:2–5, quoted in Nicholas Wolterstorff, *Until Justice and Peace Embrace* (Grand Rapids: Wm. B. Eerdmans Publishing Co., 1983), p. 102.

2. This widely known motto is quoted and marvelously interpreted in Gray Cox, *The Ways of Peace: A Philosophy of Peace as Action* (New York: Paulist Press, 1986), p. 117 and the whole of Part IV.

3. In the minds of many, however, these two critiques are at least conceptually related.

4. Cox, *The Ways of Peace,* ch. 16.

5. Roger Fisher and William Ury, *Getting to Yes: Negotiating Agreement Without Giving In* (New York: Penguin Books, 1981); cited in Cox, *The Ways of Peace,* p. 143.

6. Reinhold Niebuhr, *An Interpretation of Christian Ethics* (New York: Meridian Books, 1934, 1956), p. 169.

7. Reinhold Niebuhr, *The Nature and Destiny of Man* (New York: Charles Scribner's Sons, 1949), II, p. 261.

8. Niebuhr, *An Interpretation of Christian Ethics*, p. 167.

9. Reinhold Niebuhr, *Man's Nature and His Communities* (New York: Charles Scribner's Sons, 1965), p. 21.

10. Ibid., p. 82. Niebuhr's complete statement is: "This universal community—the dream of Hebraic Messianism and Stoic universalism, the concern of idealists from Augustine and Dante to the French utopians—although not sufficiently organized to become the concern of practical

statecraft, is brought into historical calculations and indirect concerns."

11. In addition to Cox's fuller discussion, readers interested in the techniques of concrete praxis might consult: Joan Bondurant, *The Conquest of Violence: The Gandhian Philosophy of Conflict* (Los Angeles: University of California Press, 1965); Paulo Freire, *The Pedagogy of the Oppressed* (London: Sheed & Ward, 1972); and Gene Sharp, *The Politics of Nonviolent Action* (Boston: Porter Sargent Publishers, 1973).

12. Mohandas K. Gandhi, *Hind Swaraj or Indian Home Rule* (1939), cited in Cox, *The Ways of Peace*, p. 29.

13. James E. Will, ed., *The Moral Rejection of Nuclear Deterrence* (New York: Friendship Press, 1985), p. 3.

14. Faith and Order Paper No. 85, *Church and State: Opening a New Ecumenical Discussion* (Geneva: World Council of Churches, 1978), p. 161.

15. "The Role of the World Council of Churches in International Affairs," an unpublished document (Geneva: World Council of Churches, 1986), p. 6.

16. Ibid., p. 7.

17. Ibid., p. 12.

18. Charles De Benedetti, "The American Peace Movement and the National Security State, 1941–1971," *World Affairs* 141 (Fall 1978), p. 118.

19. Cited in ibid., p. 122.

20. *PCUS General Assembly Minutes,* 1954, p. 198.

21. *Peacemaking: The Believers' Calling* (New York: General Assembly, The United Presbyterian Church U.S.A., 1980), p. 24

22. Cf. the discussion in my *The Moral Rejection of Nuclear Deterrence,* pp. 1–3.

23. General Social Survey of the National Opinion Research Center and the University of Chicago, 1980, 1982, and 1984, cited in Kenneth Wald, *Religion and Politics in the United States* (New York: St. Martin's Press, 1987), pp. 64–65.

24. Ibid., pp. 65–68.

25. Ibid., p. 80.

26. Ibid., p. 79.

27. Cited in "Religion in Public Life," *Report from the Center for Philosophy and Public Policy,* vol. 7, no. 2/3, p. 1.

28. Cf. Wald, *Religion and Politics in the United States,* p. 186.

29. Cf. Garry Wills, "Nelle's Boy: Ronald Reagan and the Disciples of Christ," *The Christian Century*, Nov. 12, 1986, pp. 1002–1006.

30. Quoted from an advertisement of the Moral Majority in Wald, *Religion and Politics in the United States,* p. 190.

31. Quoted in the *Jerusalem Post,* Oct. 28, 1983, and the *Chicago Sun-Times,* Oct. 29, 1983.

32. Cf. "The Politics of Armageddon," *Convergence* (Washington, D.C., The Christic Institute, Fall 1985), p. 3.

33. Ibid.

34. Robert Jewett, "Coming to Terms with the Doom Boom," *Quarterly Review,* vol. 4, no. 3 (Fall 1984), p. 18. Cf. also his *American Monomyth* (Garden City, N.Y.: Doubleday & Co., Anchor Press Book, 1977), *Jesus Against the Rapture* (Philadelphia: Westminster Press, 1979), and *Christian Tolerance: Paul's Message to the Modern Church* (Philadelphia: Westminster Press, 1982).

35. Jewett, "Coming to Terms with the Doom Boom," p. 20.

36. Reported in *Ecu Link* 6, Newsletter of the National Council of the Churches of Christ in the U.S.A. (February 1987), p. 5.

37. Ibid.

38. Wald, *Religion and Politics in the United States,* p. 67.

39. See the excellent article by Richard Watts, "How to Establish a Peacemaking Ministry in the Local Church," *Quarterly Review,* vol. 7, no. 1 (Spring 1987), pp. 63–75; the words cited are from p. 66.

40. Cf. Robert Jay Lifton, "The Image of 'The End of the World': A Psycho-historical View," *Michigan Quarterly Review,* XXIV:1 (Winter 1985), p. 80.

41. R. D. Laing, *The Divided Self* (Baltimore: Penguin Books, 1965), cited in an unpublished paper by Ira Chernus on "National Security and Ontological Insecurity," prepared for the American Academy of Religion, 1986.

42. Chernus, "National Security," p. 4.

43. Watts, "How to Establish a Peacemaking Ministry," p. 69.

44. Cited in Simon Harak, S.J., "One Nation, Under God: The Soteriology of SDI," p. 14, an unpublished paper prepared for the American Academy of Religion, 1987.

45. Watts, "How to Establish a Peacemaking Ministry," pp. 73–74.

46. One of the most helpful resources for this kind of comprehensive spirituality is the *Handbook for World Peacemaker Groups,* developed by the Church of the Saviour in Washington, D.C., in 1979 and revised in 1984.

47. Cited in Watts, "How to Establish a Peacemaking Ministry," pp. 74–75.

48. W. A. Williams, *The Tragedy of American Diplomacy* (New York: Delta Books, 1962), quoted by Philip Evers and Laurens Hogebrink, "The Churches in the Netherlands and Nuclear Disarmament," in *The Moral Rejection of Nuclear Deterrence,* p. 82. See also their discussion of "The Formation of a New Coalition," pp. 42–49.

49. Ibid., pp. 66 and 74.

50. Ibid., p. 55.

51. Will, ed., *The Moral Rejection of Nuclear Deterrence,* p. 226.

52. Cited in my essay on "European Peace and American Churches," *The Christian Century*, March 24, 1982, p. 330, from the *International Herald Tribune*, Nov. 18, 1981.

53. Independent Commission on Disarmament and Security, chaired by Olaf Palme, late Prime Minister of Sweden, published in the United States with the title *Common Security* (New York: Simon & Schuster, 1982).

54. *Mitteilungsblatt des Bundes* 1982, No. 5/6, p. 35, quoted by Günter Krusche, "The Political Efficacy of the Church's Responsibility for Peace in the German Democratic Republic," in *The Moral Rejection of Nuclear Deterrence,* p. 161.

55. For the Vancouver Assembly's complete "Statement on Peace and Justice," see the Appendix to *The Moral Rejection of Nuclear Deterrence,* pp. 239–246; the sentences cited are on p. 241.

56. Christian World Conference on Life and Peace: The Message, adopted April 23, 1983, Uppsala, Sweden, par. 12.

57. Lecture of Joseph Cardinal Bernardin, St. Mary of the Lake Seminary, May 6, 1983.

58. *The Interpreter*, June 1986, p. 12.

59. Agnes Cunningham, Donald Miller, and James Will, "Toward an Ecumenical Theology for Grounding Human Rights," *Soundings,* LXVII, No. 2 (Summer 1984), pp. 234–235.

60. I had the privilege of co-editing this special issue with Professor George Lucas.